To fr. ~, ~~~,

Enjoy the book !

Best wishes

Julia P. Gelardi

PAGEANT OF KINGS

The Nine Sovereigns at Edward VII's Funeral

Julia P Gelardi

AUTHOR'S NOTE

This book is part of a series, "**ROYAL CAVALCADE**," designed to give the reader a glimpse into the world of Europe's royal families and the impact their lives had on history. I've chosen to show this by focusing on a particular aspect in the fascinating, moving, and often complicated personal and political lives of royalty.

Each book is for the general reader in that those with no prior knowledge of each topic can easily read the book without feeling the need to have had prior exposure to the topic. Specialist readers - those who have extensive knowledge of the subject - can also benefit from the book because the emphasis on a particular topic can lend new or extensive light on existing knowledge.

Thank you for purchasing this book, and if have enjoyed reading this book from my series, "**ROYAL CAVALCADE**," I'd be most grateful if you could post on Amazon a brief review and read as well, other books from the series. Thanks again, and don't forget to visit my website at juliapgelardi.com.

How this Book is Arranged

The first two chapters in this book focus on the funeral of King Edward VII and the procession which took the late King's body from London to Windsor Castle, in which nine reigning European sovereigns famously took part. The book then moves on to a brief biography of each of these nine reigning monarchs.

I have structured the chapters by presenting each monarch in the order in which their reigns ended, whether by natural death, abdication, or assassination. Since King Manuel II of Portugal, though he was the youngest monarch among the group, was the first to lose his throne, I have thus placed him first in the chapters on each individual monarch. King Haakon VII of Norway is the final monarch to be highlighted because his reign, which ended in 1957, is the last of the nine sovereigns to end.

A Note on Royal Titles

The proper titles for some of the monarchs in this book are such: for kings of Greece, it is 'King of the Hellenes' or King of the Greeks; for kings of Belgium, it is 'King of the Belgians'; and for emperors of Germany it is 'German Emperor.'

For this book, I have chosen to interchange 'King of the Hellenes' with 'King of Greece'; 'King of the Belgians' with 'King of Belgium'; and 'German Emperor' with 'Emperor of Germany,' and 'Kaiser of Germany.'

TABLE OF CONTENTS

INTRODUCTION

O n May 20, 1910, the day of the funeral of Britain's King Edward VII, a special photograph was taken at Windsor Castle to commemorate an historic moment. This photograph is of nine reigning kings, resplendent in military uniform: an extraordinary record of a unique gathering, for no other visual record exists of so many reigning monarchs meeting together in one room. What makes this visual record even more exceptional is the fact that within just a decade of that photograph being taken, a tragic fate befell a number of these sovereigns. Exile, abdication or assassination awaited them. But even for those sovereigns who did not taste the bitter cup of exile or abdication or did not fall to an assassin's hand, not one escaped unscathed by tragedy of some kind – for war had cast a deep shadow upon them all, albeit in varying hues. Fate, it seemed, had in store for each of those nine sovereigns some kind of trial and tribulation.

The monarchs consist of: King Edward VII's son and successor, King George V; King Manuel II of Portugal; King George I of the Hellenes (or of Greece); King Frederick VIII of Denmark; Tsar Ferdinand I of Bulgaria; Kaiser

Wilhelm II of Germany; King Alfonso XIII of Spain; King Albert I of the Belgians; and King Haakon VII of Norway.

At the time the photograph of the nine sovereigns was taken, the order of seniority from longest to shortest by reign were as follows (with the monarchs' ages in parentheses):

King George I of the Hellenes (54 years old) – 47 years

Kaiser Wilhelm II of Germany (51 years old) – nearly 22 years

King Alfonso XIII of Spain (24 years old) – 24 years

Tsar Ferdinand I of Bulgaria (49 years old) – 21 years as ruling prince; 19 months as Tsar

King Haakon VII of Norway (37 years old) – 4.5 years

King Frederick VIII of Denmark (66 years old) – 4 years

King Manuel II of Portugal (20 years old) – 2 years

King Albert I of the Belgians (35 years old) – nearly 5 months

King George V of the United Kingdom (44 years old) – 15 days

The history and fates of the nine sovereigns varied. One was born a king while one became king at the age of sixty-two; three were elected to their thrones, all of them foreign princes who started new lives in their newly adopted countries; one became a king at the double murders of his father and elder brother; one was assassinated; and one died in a mountain-climbing accident; four lost their thrones; and five had descendants who today still reign in their respective countries.

The order in which this book unfolds is as follows: the first two chapters deal with the funeral procession of King Edward VII which took place in London on May 20, 1910 and the funeral procession at Windsor later that day (the King's body was transported by train from London to Windsor). The next chapters are devoted to each of the nine sovereigns who attended the funeral and are presented in the order in which they lost their thrones or died, and hence ended their reign. The years encompassed range from 1843 when the future King Frederick VIII of Denmark was born to 1957, the year in which King Haakon VII of Norway died – a span of 114 years.

The famous photograph of the nine sovereigns at the funeral of King Edward VII, taken at Windsor Castle, May 20, 1909.

In the photograph above, the monarch seated in the middle, King George V of the United Kingdom, takes center stage as he was son of the deceased King Edward VII and host of this special group of fellow sovereigns. Front row sitting - from left to right: King Alfonso XIII of Spain, King George V of the United Kingdom, and King Frederick VIII of Denmark. Back row standing – from left to right: King Haakon VII of Norway; Tsar Ferdinand I of Bulgaria; King Manuel II of Portugal; Kaiser Wilhelm II of Germany; King George I of Greece; and Belgium's King Albert I.

The sovereigns were related in varying degrees. In terms of immediate relations, King George V was the nephew of Greece's King George I and King Frederick VIII of Denmark (who were brothers), and a first cousin of Kaiser Wilhelm II of Germany. A first cousin of George V was married to King Alfonso XIII of Spain, while King George V's own sister was married to King Haakon VII of Norway. King Haakon VII of Norway was also the son of King Frederick VIII of Denmark.

Three monarchs who were not in attendance at King Edward VII's funeral were Tsar Nicholas II of Russia, King Victor Emmanuel II of Italy, and Emperor Franz Joseph I of Austria-Hungary. The Tsar was represented by his mother, the Dowager Empress Marie Feodorovna (a sister-in-law of the late Edward VII) and his brother, Grand Duke Michael. King Victor Emmanuel II was represented by the Duke of Aosta. The aged Emperor Franz Joseph I was represented by his heir, the Archduke Franz Ferdinand, whose assassination in 1914, triggered the start of World War I.

Chapter 1. The Most Remarkable Gathering

The Procession of Nine Kings

Never had London witnessed such an impressive sight, a splendid display of British pageantry – a somber but brilliant farewell to a well-loved monarch. It was an unprecedented ceremony witnessed by densely packed crowds estimated at a staggering 2.5 million plus souls. They poured into the British capital, by tram, train, and underground from all parts of London and its surrounding suburbs as well as differing parts of the United Kingdom. Countless people packed into Piccadilly, Hyde Park, the Mall, Marble Arch, and other well-known parts of London. They had had come to mourn their dead King and nearly all were dressed in black.

The event was the funeral procession of Britain's King Edward VII which took place on May 20, 1910. One of the most arresting images found on that bright, warm day was the sight of nine reigning monarchs following the gun-carriage carrying the remains of the late King.

It was "the most remarkable gathering of monarchs ever seen in this city of pageants," declared a British newspaper of the day. These monarchs were in London to pay their respects to one of their own. Fourteen days before, the curtain descended upon the life of the colorful, energetic, and immensely popular King Edward VII, who died at the age of sixty-eight at Buckingham Palace. Edward, the son and heir of the legendary Queen Victoria whom he succeeded as monarch in January 1901, reigned for a mere nine years. And yet Edward VII had made his mark on the world stage and his reign and the subsequent four years prior to the outbreak of World War I has come to be known as the Edwardian Era. Upon King Edward's death, he was succeeded by his second son, who became King George V.

Despite his penchant for overeating, smoking copious cigars, as well as his notorious philandering and marital scandals, Edward had become a popular monarch. He had been a

7

conscientious sovereign, looking out for the interests of the United Kingdom, particularly when it came to foreign relations with other European powers. Moreover, his bonhomie meant that Edward possessed an ability to charm and disarm others. Consequently, when the King died, he was genuinely mourned by his fellow countrymen. None, though, mourned King Edward VII more than his son, King George V. In a tribute to his father, George V wrote to a friend: "I was simply devoted to him & consulted him in everything, we were more like brothers, he was my best friend. So you can understand how terribly I miss him & long for his advice in the new life which I am now beginning with its many responsibilities."

King Edward VII's death shocked his subjects for they were under the impression that having recently returned from Biarritz, France, the King had come home "invigorated and refreshed by his stay abroad." And so when the news was announced that the King had died, it was received by the British people, according to William Boyd Carpenter, the Bishop of Ripon and chaplain to Queen Victoria, "with profound and startled emotion" because Edward VII's death had come with "bewildering suddenness." It was "a national loss: it stirred our emotions." Consequently, "an unbroken flood of eulogy" and "widespread testimony to his work and worth as a king" flowed forth.

The eulogies were genuine and effusive. "Throughout the whole land - throughout the Empire – a sense of deepest sorrow is felt in the loss of a King who had endeared himself to a larger number of his fellow human beings than any man living," wrote the Rev. P.M. Phillips of Wesley. "The suddenness of the blow and its staggering effect on the entire nation are such that we cannot yet grasp the significance of the event." And from the pen of another clergyman, the Rev. E. Carrington of Nottingham, the emotional impact of the King's passing could be gleaned: "The nation has been plunged into a loss tragically sudden by the death of the King. We are all stricken and bewildered. He had proved a great constitutional monarch … In our nation's history he will be known as Edward the Peacemaker – a title almost as noteworthy as that of Edward the Confessor."

Those who had personally known Edward VII were full of praise for him. The Liberal politician and British courtier, Viscount Esher, recorded that, "he had an instinct for statecraft which carried him straight to the core of a great problem, without deep thought or profound knowledge of the subject. He had one supreme gift, and this was his unerring judgment of men – and women." Esher was generous in his assessment, stating that, "I have known all the great men of my time in this land of ours, and many beyond it. He was the most kingly of them all."

Princess Daisy of Pless, the English-born aristocrat, who married into one of the wealthiest German aristocratic families in Germany also had high praise for King Edward VII: "The place of England and the British Empire was assured and unassailable … He needed neither crowns, nor clanking swords, nor Horse or Foot Guards to remind people that he not only occupied the greatest throne in the world – ruling over one-fifth of the whole earth – but that, by virtue of his own personality, he was the first gentleman in Europe – or any-where." Another tribute came from a friend of the late King's, Baron Suffield, who wrote that: "He was rightly called the *Peacemaker*; *Well-Beloved* is another expression that rises inevitably to the minds of all who knew him … King Edward had a naturally sweet and gentle disposition … but all other attributes were secondary to his strong sense of right and fair play." And Sir Frederick Ponsonby who had served King Edward VII as his Assistant Private Secretary, noted that, "with King Edward's passing we lost a lovable, wayward and human monarch. He was one who came to decisions by instinct and not by logic, and rarely made a mistake in his judgment of men."

One individual who did not share in the glowing tributes to the late King Edward VII was the German Emperor, Wilhelm II. Kaiser Wilhelm feuded with the man who had been his maternal uncle. Wilhelm believed that his Uncle Bertie wanted nothing more than to encourage other European nations to side against Germany and encircle her. In 1907, the Kaiser infamously declared of his uncle: "He is a Satan; you can hardly believe what a Satan he is." No such outburst, however, came out of Kaiser Wilhelm, the "possessor of the least inhibited tongue in Europe," throughout the obsequies for the late British King. In fact, Wilhelm II acted with restrained respect during the final farewells to the man who was his uncle, nemesis, and the sovereign of the largest empire in history.

Not long after the King died, preparations were underway for a funeral suited to a king and emperor, for not only had Edward been King of the United Kingdom of Great Britain and Ireland, he had also been Emperor of India. The King himself had been a man of consequence, exerting his influence upon the international stage. And so, it came as no surprise that the obsequies would be memorable. The funeral had all the makings of a great state occasion as befitting a royal to whom "ceremonial majesty came easily, pageantry was for him the breath of life." Indeed, "throughout his life Edward VII had been keenly appreciative of the pomp and circumstance of his royal position, and it was by a singular stroke of irony that the greatest state pageant in which he" took part was "his own funeral."

In a funeral of this magnitude persons of consequence were invited to attend, meaning that reigning kings were at the top of the list. As soon as the invitations were sent, numerous monarchs, a number of whom had been related to King Edward, made their way to England. "Crowned heads with their suites and families arrived by train. Aides-de-camp were waiting for them at Dover and Victoria [train station in London], organized with the same precision as at the time of the Coronation [of Edward VII]." In the end, nine reigning sovereigns paid their last respects to the late Edward VII. Thanks to the presence of these sovereigns, the stately funeral "marked, or seemed to mark, an apogee in the long history of Europe's reigning houses."

The reigning monarchs who attended the funereal ceremonies for King Edward VII in London and Windsor consisted of the late King's son, King George V; Edward VII's son-in-law,

King Haakon VII of Norway; the late King's brothers-in-law, King Frederick VIII of Denmark and King George I of Greece; Edward VII's nephew, Kaiser Wilhelm II of Germany; the late King's nephew-by-marriage, King Alfonso XIII of Spain; Tsar Ferdinand I of Bulgaria; King Manuel II of Portugal; and King Albert I of the Belgians.

The late King's body had lain in state at the historic Westminster Hall, the oldest building in Parliament, dating back to the 10th century. It was the site of the trials of Anne Boleyn, St. Thomas More, and King Charles I. But this time, history of a different kind unfolded. Here, countless mourners dressed in black - the late King's subjects - filed past in silent respect. When the Hall was opened to the public, some 40,000 people were already waiting, with the line extending from Westminster Hall to Vauxhall Bridge. At one point, "the queue was four miles long and six abreast – an orderly respectful human procession, snaking around the streets of Westminster like the black ink that bordered the nation's mourning newspapers." The heavy downpour of rain did not stop the seemingly endless queues from forming, for here was the people's opportunity to file past Edward VII's flag-draped coffin and pay their last respects.

Royalty, too, paid their respects to the late monarch. Twenty-year-old King Manuel II of

Portugal stopped late one night at Westminster Hall accompanied by his ambassador to London, the Marquis of Soveral, one of King Edward's good friends, muttering repeatedly: "This is too awful." Another royal mourner was Germany's flamboyant Emperor, Wilhelm II, whose relationship with his late uncle had been infused with suspicion and acrimony. On the day he visited Westminster Hall, Wilhelm II was on his best behavior and could not help but be impressed with what he saw. The Kaiser left a vivid picture in words of what he saw and experienced:

> *King George drove me to Westminster Hall, where the gorgeously decorated coffin, reposed upon a towering catafalque, guarded by household troops, troops of the line, and detachments from the Indian and Colonial contingents, all in the traditional attitude of mourning – heads bowed, hands crossed over the butts and hilts of their reversed arms. The old, gray hall, covered by its great Gothic wooden ceiling, towered imposingly over the catafalque, lighted merely by a few rays of the sun filtering through narrow windows. One ray flooded the magnificent coffin of the King, surmounted by the English crown, and made marvelous play with the colors of the stones adorning it.*

> *Past the catafalque, countless*
> *throngs of men, women, and children, of all*
> *classes and strata in the nation passed in*
> *silence, many with hands folded to bid*
> *farewell to him who had been so popular as*
> *a ruler. A most impressive picture, in its*
> *marvelous medieval setting.*

At one point, the Kaiser and King George V solemnly shook hands after Wilhelm prayed by the bier of Edward VII. The scene impressed those who witnessed it. On the evening before the funeral procession in London was to take place, a banquet was given by King George V at Buckingham Palace for his distinguished guests – "a veritable wake" was how Theodore Roosevelt, one of the guests, described it. During the course of the evening, a member of the British royal family said to Wilhelm II: "Your handshake with our King is all over London. The people are deeply impressed by it and take it as a good omen for the future."

"That is the sincerest wish of my heart," replied the Kaiser.

During this same dinner, Theodore Roosevelt met with and spoke to many of the illustrious guests present, including the nine reigning sovereigns. Roosevelt thought Tsar Ferdinand I of Bulgaria "a very competent fellow, but with some unattractive traits." Interestingly, Roosevelt thought "all the other sovereigns were angry with him [Tsar Ferdinand I] because he had suddenly christened himself czar instead of king, which they regarded as bumptious."

The night before the funeral rain and thunderstorms pelted the British capital. But the day of the funeral procession, Friday, May 20th, in which the King's body was taken from London to Windsor Castle for burial, turned out bright and warm, with the sun shining. Anticipation had built toward this day, for "the funeral was the supreme moment of the Edwardian cavalcade." London was swathed in a sea of solemn and somber colors. The late King "had a horror of black" and so "the streets and the monuments were draped in purple. All the same, within a few hours of his death, it was impossible to find a foot of crape in the smallest little shop in the kingdom, and cargo ships had to be sent to Germany to collect more."

Large crowds formed early. "The noble thoroughfare at Marble Arch was practically impassable," noted one newspaper of the day, "and this before the early morning trains had begun to discharge their thousands." Innumerable people wanted to find a spot from which to view the procession which wound its way from Westminster

Hall to Paddington Station. One newspaper reporter recorded that:

> ... *the greatest crushes seemed to congregate in Whitehall and Piccadilly ... Whitehall was practically impassable at seven o'clock, and long before the time of the procession the road was blocked to Trafalgar-square ... At every conceivable inlet the crowd was being headed off to the north; they vanished up side streets, or were driven like sheep into the wide spaces in the Park [Hyde Park], and saw nothing more.*

Once one secured a spot, the waiting for the actual procession became an exercise in patience, for:

> *It was terribly hot on the sunny side of the streets. The people on the pavements waited patiently with a burning sun full on them, envying those who enjoyed the grateful shade. But in spite of the intense heat and the trial of the long waiting there was a wonderful spirit of kindliness ... Everybody was willing to pass the women and children to the front, and many a man sacrificed his own view of the procession.*

When the appointed hour of the procession neared, "all ears were strained to catch the first deep boom of the minute-gun which was to announce the beginning of the King's last journey through the capital he had loved …"

The funeral procession of King Edward VII through the streets of London attracted a tremendous number of mourners and spectators. People jostled for prime viewing spots. The interest was so great that according to one contemporary report the people "not only packed the line of march, but filled all the side streets and covered the roofs of houses and even fought for position at points where there was no possibility of obtaining a view of the pageant" so that "by dawn the streets were jammed." Sir Frederick Ponsonby recalled that "the crowd was the largest I have ever seen." *The Daily Telegraph & Courier* reported that: "At some places the multitude was so vast that from a distance it did not seem to consist of people; it could have been called an element." Moreover, "everywhere the crowd is enormous, incredible, fantastic. The stands erected along the route have almost disappeared beneath the swarming mass of humanity." These stands afforded some of the best views of the funeral procession. Demand was high for these places. The steep price of £100 per person (approximately £8,000 today) did not deter individuals from snapping up these coveted positions.

As impressive as the funeral procession turned out to be, just as impressive were the number of people who flocked to London on that momentous day of King Edward VII's funeral. In its coverage of the funeral, The *Daily Telegraph & Courier* left a memorable account of just how densely packed the streets of London were, and how the public "came out not in battalions or divisions, but in armies:

> *They filled every corner of the wide footways, and they were worthy of being likened to an army, for their discipline was superb. They had no leaders to command them, and required none, and the fatigue occasioned by long hours of waiting in hot sunshine did not cause anyone to forget that the day was one of national mourning. Wherever you looked you were confronted with a dense mass in unbroken black. Towards Westminster, above the wide, grey walls of the abbey which was misted over with a faint blue haze, one saw the roof of that Gothic fane packed with people. In the opposite direction a solid block of spectators appeared to cover Trafalgar-square, and you realised how immense must be the multitude which could not get within visual range of the procession. On the pathways within the police cordons it was generally difficult and often impossible to move. The banks of*

*people in the streets formed the biggest
proportion, but not the whole, of the
spectators. In the Government offices every
window space was full, and in the stands
which had been built within the grey
hoardings enclosing the public buildings
there were many hundreds of privileged Civil
servants.*

"Every window" on the procession route
was occupied, noted one newspaper reporter, and
"people crowded on the roofs of houses, and stood
packed for hours on specially erected stands." To
control the vast crowds, 35,000 soldiers and
thousands more policemen were stationed
throughout the route of the funeral cortege. The
crush of people and the intense heat coupled with
the long waits were more than enough to stretch the
endurance of many. Hundreds of mourners
collapsed. A number of soldiers standing guard
along the route fainted and fell flat on their faces.
The ambulance corps were kept busy dealing with
people overcome by heat and exhaustion. Water
bearers were at hand to aid people and horses.
Police and nurses attended to the casualties. Despite
the hardships they had to endure, the behavior of
the large crowds was impeccable. People helped
each other, ceding ground to the less fortunate and
aiding them. One particularly poignant example

occurred when "one officer, bearing shattered silken colours – silent witness of great events at Sebastopol and Inkerman [in the Crimean War] – was overcome by the heat, and had to relinquish his proud position. A private stepped from the ranks, took up the colours, and promptly stood at attention before his company."

For those fortunate enough to catch a glimpse of the funeral procession, they were not disappointed for it amounted to a spectacle "of indescribable magnificence and dignity." It was a "ceremony almost unprecedented in the annals of Royal obsequies," so declared *The West Coast News*, a newspaper from the far corner of the Empire, New Zealand. This was echoed by Britain's *Western Daily Press*, which stated that: "Nothing in recorded history is comparable to the scenes of solemn grandeur which … attended the funeral of King Edward the Seventh … They paled even the majestic scenes witnessed in connection with the obsequies of Queen Victoria." And "great as was the gathering of Monarchs and Princes at the funeral of Queen Victoria," that of King Edward VII's funeral "was one that could hardly conceivably be surpassed."

Indeed, this "brilliant, glittering assembly of illustrious Kings and Princes" as one British newspaper noted, was unprecedented, adding grandiloquently that: "It is a procession not only striking in its magnificence, but infinitely more so by reason of its significance. Here are the nations of the earth gathered together in the persons of their rulers. Laid low for the time are jealousies; banished are the rivalries of Empires; there is room but for one rivalry in this great day of tribulation – the rivalry of sorrowing homage to the departed Peacemaker."

Besides the splendid pageantry that involved tens of thousands of soldiers and military officers, and the impressively large crowds, it was the presence of the nine sovereigns that added a special dignity and unique luster to the funeral of King Edward VII. The nine monarchs constituted a truly exceptional gathering. The sovereigns had gathered in the Quadrangle of Buckingham Palace to begin their procession through London. It was a scene of "extreme magnificence and interest," declared the *Lancashire Evening Post* in its account of the event, which went on to describe in detail the scene in the Palace Quadrangle:

> *The King of Spain, wearing the uniform of a British General and the Order of the Garter, was one of the first to appear on the scene ... The King of Portugal, looking very smart in a Portuguese uniform*

with heavy gold epaulettes, was one of the first residents within the Palace to appear in the Quadrangle and mount his charger. A little later came the German Emperor. His Majesty wore the uniform of a British Field Marshal, and carried the baton, the sign of that rank. The King of Bulgaria's figure as he mounted his horse in the Quadrangle was a very striking one. His Majesty did not appear in British uniform, but in that of his own army, the headdress of which is a remarkable turban. The King of Greece rode beside his brother, the King of Denmark. Another notable figure in the striking group was the King of Norway. Altogether there were nine kings in the parade ground, if it might be so called, and Royal Princes by the dozen.

As King Edward VII's widow, Queen Alexandra, sister of Denmark's King Frederick VIII and Greece's King George I, entered her glass coach, the sovereigns saluted her. Seated next to Queen Alexandra was her sister, the Dowager Empress Marie Feodorovna of Russia. The two sisters, heavily gowned and veiled in black, harbored an intense dislike for the most famous of the royal mourners just ahead of them, Germany's

Kaiser Wilhelm II, astride a white charger in his uniform of a British Field Marshal.

Meanwhile, countless ordinary Britons who had packed London's streets were awash in a myriad of emotions. They mourned, but were also filled with awe, excitement, and wonder. One reporter was struck by the reverent silence, describing it as "magic, prodigious, superhuman. This silence is almost more terrible than a tumult; it has a subjugating majesty. An ineffable emotion penetrates you, because you feel it all around; it exhales from the vast soul of the people." But when words were exchanged, they were done in *sotto voce* so that "all conversation was carried on in a subdued key. In giving commands to their troops, the officers spoke in hushed tones, and the police, in moving people from places where they were becoming too closely packed, almost whispered their advice to pass along this way or that way." Overall, however, "a hushed" and "deadly silence" pervaded "save for the booming of the gun" and "the orders to the troops given in undertones" to stand at "Attention" or "Rest on your arms reversed."

All eyes from the vast crowds who could see the panoply were glued to the spectacle that unfolded before them as the royal cavalcade proceeded from Buckingham Palace to Westminster

Hall and onwards to Paddington Station. Upon their arrival at Westminster Hall, King George V and Kaiser Wilhelm II dismounted from their horses and accompanied Queen Alexandra and her daughter, Princess Victoria, into the vast medieval Hall. The rest of the monarchs remained mounted on their horses. Minutes later, King George V, Kaiser Wilhelm II, Queen Alexandra, and Princess Victoria, emerged from the Hall, watching as King Edward VII's coffin, covered with the Royal Standard, was borne on the shoulders of bare-headed Guardsmen. The coffin was placed on a gun-carriage and then the Crown and Scepter were laid on top of the coffin. The procession then began, and "nearly every bell in London began tolling and the air seemed to vibrate with their sonorous tones of sorrow."

As the procession slowly proceeded, massed military bands from branches of the British armed forces along with those of territories of the British Empire played funeral marches. The military detachments were especially striking in the image they left the crowds. "Gorgeous uniforms and splendid martial bearing captivated the crowd," noted a reporter, "and when the officers of the navies and armies of nine Continental countries were joined by the military attachés of the foreign Embassies a touch of brilliance was given to the

cortège, which made a profound impression."
Moreover, "dragoons, cuirassiers, and hussars,
magnificently horsed, belonging to the regiments
which bear the names of British monarchs in their
titles" bore colorful testament to the history of
military accomplishments of the British forces. The
extent of this parade of militaria can be gleaned
from the fact that: "From Downing-street, to the
Horse Guards were marshalled the representatives
of the Royal Navy, Royal Marine Artillery, and
Royal Marine Light Infantry and the vanguard of
the procession must have been half a mile ahead of
them."

As each minute passed, guns reverberated.
Throughout the processional route that wound its
way from Westminster Hall to Paddington Station,
the mourning colors of black and purple
predominated. Façades and balconies were draped
in these colors, some in heavy festoons and folding
cascades that gave them "all the grandeur of Royal
baldachins." Thousands of wreaths composed of
laurel and oak leaves, cypress, and ivy, some made
by schoolchildren, embellished the railings of
Green Park and Hyde Park. Troops also lined the
capital's streets – "by Whitehall, the Mall, St.
James's Street, Piccadilly, Hyde Park, Edgware
Road, and Oxford and Cambridge Terraces, to
Paddington Station, minute-guns were fired, and

the vast crowds unconvered [their heads] and observed a reverent silence. Their order and demeanour," noted one contemporary account, "were admirable."

Nearly an hour after the procession had begun, the gun-carriage and the royal mourners behind it had arrived at Whitehall and as one reporter noted, "threaded its way amidst an extraordinary silence. The mournful roll of the muffled drums, the haunting strains of Beethoven's funeral march, the occasional jingling of accoutrements, and the steady crunch of hoofs upon the gravel were the only sounds to be heard beyond the ear-deafening boom of the guns and the melancholy clanging of the great bell. Women wept unrestrainedly but silently. Men vainly endeavoured to hide their emotion as the solemn and majestic spectacle unfolded before their gaze."

As the body of King Edward VII – the 'Uncle of Europe' was ceremoniously taken through London, eyes were glued to the high and mighty monarchs who followed on horseback the gun carriage bearing the King's coffin. Heading the mourners were King George V flanked by his uncle, the Duke of Connaught, and his cousin, Kaiser Wilhelm II. Behind them rode King Haakon VII of Norway, King George I of the Hellenes, and King Alfonso XIII of Spain. Behind these monarchs rode Tsar Ferdinand I of Bulgaria, King Frederick VIII of Denmark, and King Manuel II of Portugal. The row behind consisted of the Hereditary Prince of the Ottoman Empire, King Albert I of the Belgians, and Archduke Franz Ferdinand.

"The kingly group" proved to be "the supreme point of interest" to many according to one reporter who watched the procession, "but the Monarchs and Princes followed one another so closely that ... there were few who were clearly identified by the onlookers. No one, however, failed to recognise the stately figure of the German Emperor, riding by the side of King George, but always carefully maintaining his position a little to the rear; and the young King of Spain, too, attracted every eye."

The funeral procession was a spectacle so majestic and grand that superlative descriptions of the ceremonies abounded. A contemporary description of the event captured in poetic and highly descriptive terms the obsequies – "the magnificent solemnities of a funeral which resembled a triumph." Moreover:

> *It was not one nation but all nations; not one people, but all peoples that saluted the Peacemaker as he passed the last threshold of the world ... And London made*

for the departed a worthy wreath; the town,
assuming the severity of an immense temple,
offered an incomparable spectacle of
religious meditation.

As though by enchantment the vast
metropolis was transformed. For a day it
ceased to be the great capital of labour and
commerce; it forgot all its cares and all its
business, and retired into reverent seclusion.
For a moment in the huge city there was no
other movement except the slow advance of a
cortège which wound its splendours through
mourning multitudes.

Hard is the task of giving an
impression of this funeral day. In the eyes it
has left a confusion of magnificence, and in
the soul a medley of emotions. It all appears
too vast to be described.

Years later, in her famous work, *The Guns
of August*, the historian Barbara Tuchman captured
the flavor of the event and left a vivid description of
King Edward VII's funeral in the opening chapter
of her book:

So gorgeous was the spectacle on
the May morning of 1910 when nine kings
rode in the funeral of Edward VII of England
that the crowds, waiting in hushed and
black-clad awe, could not keep back gasps of

admiration. In scarlet and blue and green and purple, three by three the sovereigns rode through the palace gates, with plumed helmets, gold braid, crimson sashes, and jeweled orders flashing in the sun. After them came five heirs apparent, forty more imperial or royal highnesses, seven queens – four dowagers and three regnant – and a scattering of special ambassadors from uncrowned countries. Together they represented seventy nations in the greatest assemblage of royalty and rank ever gathered in one place and, of its kind, the last. The muffled tongue of Big Ben tolled nine by the clock as the cortege left the palace, but on history's clock it was sunset, and the sun of the old world was setting in a dying blaze of splendor never to be seen again.

The royal funeral was indeed a ceremony of splendor that was not to be seen again. This was in large part due to the presence of nine reigning European sovereigns. Such a meeting of kings was never to be matched; and though no one present to watch the funeral procession of Edward VII in London on that May morning of 1910, could have imagined what was in store in just four years with the outbreak of the Great War, a sense of living through an epic moment permeated those who witnessed the glories unfold. From the doyen of monarchs, Kaiser Wilhelm II of Germany, to one of the youngest official mourners, such as Prince Edward, son and heir of the new British King, the obsequies of Edward VII made a powerful impact.

In his naval cadet uniform, fifteen-year-old Prince Edward and his younger brother, Prince Albert (the future Kings Edward VIII and George VI) followed their father and the other royal mourners. Years later, the former King Edward VIII, in his memoirs, recalled that it was "a hot and sultry day." The young Prince was especially moved by the sight of so many mourners and how "a hush lay over the dense, perspiring and fainting crowds in the London streets, broken only by the sounds of the horses' hoofs and the mournful funeral marches of the massed military bands."

The fifty-one-year old German Emperor was just as struck by the obsequies as his teenaged great-nephew, Prince Edward, had been. In recalling the funeral procession in London, the Kaiser wrote eloquently of the scene:

> *As I rode through London behind the coffin of my uncle I was a witness of the tremendous and impressive demonstration of grief on the part of the vast multitude – estimated at several millions – on streets,*

balconies, and roofs, every one of whom was clad in black, every man of whom stood with bared head, among all of whom reigned perfect order and absolute stillness. Upon this somber, solemn background the files of British soldiers stood out all the more gorgeously. In splendid array marched the battalions of the English Guards: Grenadiers, Scots Guards, Coldstreams, Irish Guards – in their perfectly-fitting coats, white leather facings, and heavy bearskin head-gear; all picked troops of superb appearance and martial bearing, a joy to any man with the heart of a soldier. And all the troops lining the path of the funeral cortège stood in the attitude of mourning already described.

Though nine reigning sovereigns were present at the funeral of King Edward VII, three did not attend. Tsar Nicholas II, along with Italy's King Vittorio Emanuele III, and Austria-Hungary's Emperor Franz Joseph I were notably absent from the funeral ceremonies. Nevertheless, the Tsar of Russia was represented by his brother, the Grand Duke Michael. The King of Italy had sent his cousin, the Duke of Aosta, to represent him, while Emperor Franz Joseph I had sent his nephew and heir, Archduke Franz Ferdinand, to represent him.

Other senior royal personages who did attend included the Prince Consort of the Netherlands; the Crown Princes of the Ottoman Empire, Bavaria, Greece, Romania, and Serbia; and an array of other royal personages and representatives of many nations.

The funeral cortege consisted of an impressive array of military men in their uniforms - colorful and glinting in the May sunlight. Even those who stood guard over the crowds left an indelible impression. Among them, were detachments of the Household Cavalry who were especially striking. For as one eyewitness wrote, "as the sun scintillated on their breastplates and the wind tossed their plumes the whole picture, framed in a mass of silent humanity, was one which left a deep impression." No less impressive was the sight of Field Marshals Lord Kitchener, Earl Roberts, and Evelyn Wood as they rode with the other illustrious mourners. From Westminster Hall they processed in slow cadence to the wail of bagpipes and muffled drumbeats.

Behind the gun-carriage pulled by eight horses, followed the late King's rider-less caparisoned charger, as was the custom in military funerals. The boots of the charger's late master were placed in reverse in its stirrups. It was a powerful reminder of the absence of the King. But what touched the innumerable mourners who lined the route was the sight of what followed King Edward's rider-less horse: his white fox terrier, Caesar. The dog was Edward VII's constant companion in the twilight years of his life. In the funeral procession, Caesar, on a leash, was accompanied by a kilted soldier. Caesar's participation in the funeral cortege made such an impact that a contemporary publication reported that, "the appearance of the dog on this occasion gave to the public as a whole a great thrill of emotion second only to that felt at the moment of the passing of the body." Not everyone, however, was pleased that Caesar had been accorded a special place in the cortege. The German Emperor had reputedly resented the fact that he, along with his fellow sovereigns, were accorded places behind Caesar in the procession. Nevertheless, Kaiser Wilhelm did not make a scene about Caesar's precedence and acquiesced to the terrier's important role in the procession.

The fact that Caesar the terrier was given a prominent role in the procession along with the crowned heads of Europe added a personal touch to a royal funeral that was marked by much pomp and pageantry. The crowds were deeply impressed by so much of what unfolded before them – the sights and sounds of a moving cavalcade, a montage of military precision which saw companies of soldiers marching with their heads bowed and arms reversed. The colorful uniforms, the silence, the firing of guns by the minute, Chopin and Beethoven's funeral marches, the late King's coffin, his rider-less charger, little Caesar, the mourning family who happened to be the people's royal family – all melded into a magnificent panoply. But what most stood out was the sight of the nine monarchs. The crowds, aware that they might likely never again see such a pageant of kings, watched King George V ride past, "erect and almost statuesque." And as "the great Monarchs of Europe" rode past the countless mourners, the kings were "silently regarded" by many of the crowds "with curious but most intense interest." Such were the conclusions of the *Western Daily Press*, observations echoed by *The Daily Telegraph & Courier* which stated that the public "displayed extraordinary interest in the Royal mourners, and after King George, the Kaiser, and the Duke of Connaught had passed the keen desire to identify each of the remaining Kings and Princes loosened the tongues of the people…" Indeed, the people had murmured and exchanged impressions, telling others "of the splendour of the Royal pageant."

The presence of so many reigning monarchs was, as *The Illustrated London News* told its readers: "The Tribute of Great Kings to a Great King." The presence of these monarchs along with the other royals amounted to "the most remarkable company of Reigning Sovereigns and Princes which has ever been seen in the world's history." The monarchs' presence, lent an impressive luster to the event, prompting one American newspaper to declare: "It was the most imposing funeral the world has ever seen…"

Chapter 2. An Exceptional Group

Funeral procession of the late King Edward VII:
the Royal Carriages

Not long before noon, the royal procession, which had taken two hours to traverse three miles, arrived at London's Paddington Station. As mourners watched the arrival of the gun-carriage with the coffin, "a wave of silent emotion swept over" the crowds, "but not a sound escaped them," noted a reporter who witnessed the scene. "They sat as still as statues, and watched the King and the Kaiser go by each with stern faces…" Upon their arrival at Paddington, the nine sovereigns rode past the gun-carriage and then dismounted from their horses, all the while the "solemn dirge" of the Dead March" from *Saul* "crashed out "in heavy, hearth-throbbing cadences."

After the coffin was reverently carried into one of the train carriages, and the assorted royals had embarked, all was set to go. Just before noon, the signal was given for the royal train to depart. It did so slowly to the strains again of the "Dead March." And as the train containing the body of the late King left Paddington, it was evident to all that "London had taken its last farewell of King Edward."

At Windsor, some twenty-two miles to the west of London, a shining sun, deep blue sky, and diaphanous clouds greeted residents and visitors. At the town's Great Western Railway Station, trains began arriving carrying distinguished guests from Britain and around the world. A brilliant panoply unfolded as these guests along with members of the military gathered in their white and black plumed hats and uniforms of blues and reds, joined by a contingent of Yeoman of the Guard in their distinct colorful Tudor uniforms and halberds.

The task of conveying an exceptionally large number of distinguished guests from London to Windsor required elaborate and precise arrangements be made and executed. From Paddington, five special trains were used to transport the most important guests. The trains arrived at ten-minute intervals at Windsor starting at 11:30 a.m.

The presence of so many important guests presented a challenge when it came to protecting them. Railway officials guarded the entire railway line, including sidings, level crossings, bridges, and footpaths all the way from Paddington to Windsor. And according to one account: "Although the public route in Windsor does not pass through more than a quarter of a mile of public thoroughfares, nearly a thousand police were on duty in addition to the military…"

When guns stationed at the Long Walk boomed and the bells from Windsor Castle began to toll, all knew that the royal train was minutes way from arriving. After half an hour's journey, the royal train arrived at Windsor's Great Western Railway Station whose platforms were draped in purple mourning cloth and carpeted in crimson and purple. The military men set to accompany the royal coffin to its final resting place of St. George's Chapel, within the grounds of Windsor Castle, offered an impressive sight. They consisted of Bluejackets, enlisted men of the Royal Navy, in their blue uniforms and white straw hats; the Second Battalion of the Scots Guards; and the

King's Company of the Grenadier Guards, every single one of them towering over 6 feet.

Within seconds of the royal train coming to a standstill at the platform, the King's Company of the Grenadier Guards stood with reversed arms, uniformed soldiers stood in salute, and civilian men uncovered their heads.

The first of the royals to set foot onto the platform at Windsor's station were King George V, the Duke of Connaught, and Kaiser Wilhelm. Immediately following them came the monarchs of Norway, Greece, Spain, Bulgaria, Denmark, and Portugal, followed by other royals including Queen Alexandra, and Dowager Empress Marie. No words were exchanged as the royals alighted from the train. "The silence," according to an eyewitness, "became oppressive, and the hot rays of the sun seemed to be striking down into a dead spectacle. It was a muteness which made one feel momentarily faint." This same eagle-eyed newspaper reporter noted how Queen Alexandra's eyes "were full of tears" while the Kaiser "looked on, and every moment it seemed as if the lines of his face would become sterner in the effort to restrain a tremendous emotion."

Queen Alexandra, King George V, the Kaiser, along with the other monarchs, watched non-commissioned officers of the Guards carry the royal coffin from the train unto the waiting gun-carriage. The late King's aides-de-camp and equerries then placed the Crown, Orb, and Scepter, and Insignia of the Order of the Garter atop the royal coffin, still covered by the Royal Standard. And then the funeral procession began, executed with the same military precision and aplomb which had characterized the London part of the funeral. Once the word was sent forth that all was in readiness:

> *... quite suddenly, the rattle of drums, first very low and tender, swelling into a magnificent volume of sound, preceded the crash of the brass instruments as the first bars of the Funeral March were heard amid booming guns and tolling bells.*
>
> *A shrill whistle from the commander of the sailors and the lifting of a hand made them strain at the white rope attached to the gun-carriage, on which was the Royal coffin. Thirteen rows of sailors, eight abreast, pulled, and five rows steadied the carriage from behind. Easily it moved, and as the band struck up a higher note in the street, the procession started. Solemnly it passed through the historic streets, amid tense silence, and proceeded on its way up the Long Walk to St. George's Chapel.*

Densely packed crowds, silent and somber in black, watched just as in London, to witness history. One contemporary newspaper report explained to its readers that:

> *Never in the history of Windsor had such a dense crowd wedged itself in so small a compass. Although the route in the public street was only a quarter of a mile, there were at least 50,000 people present. Every window, every balcony, and every roof were packed to their utmost capacity. Below was a seething mass. Some of the spectators took up their positions before six o'clock. By ten o'clock the streets were almost impassible, and still they came. For the people's safety it became necessary to stop vehicular traffic in the street, and then ensued a great struggle for places.*

Again, as in London, "as the hours passed, the strain of waiting in the scorching rays of the sun began to tell," and numerous individuals fainted and had to be attended to by the St. John Ambulance Brigade.

Those who witnessed the funeral procession at Windsor, "beheld a magnificent spectacle in a glorious setting" with "the great battlemented walls of the Castle" and the color and spectacle of the military and royal personages file past in fine precision. Owing to the narrow parts on Windsor's High Street, members of the public who were fortunate enough to watch the procession pass them from these parts were offered a close, almost intimate view of the royal cavalcade. From the mourners' vantage point, they saw in close proximity, King George V, keeping his emotions in check, flanked by the German Emperor and the Duke of Connaught. Behind them marched the two oldest sons of George V, and then came the other eight monarchs, various royals, and eminent mourners. Following them were Queen Alexandra and the Dowager Empress of Russia in one carriage. Further behind in another carriage were Queen Mary; her daughter; and Queen Maud of Norway, who was Edward VII's youngest daughter.

Years later, the Duke of Windsor, the former King Edward VIII, wrote of how: "Bluejackets dragged it [the gun-carriage] slowly up the hill to St. George's Chapel: the long funeral procession followed on foot." The Duke and his young siblings had found the funeral "rather overpowering … even a little eerie."

Many who witnessed the funeral procession were impressed by the remarkable sights and sounds. "Such a spectacle – such a tableau – of the fighting forces and the regal and princely magnificence of the nations of the world has not been seen gathered together within so small a canvas for many years. And the sunlight, moreover, added to the splendour of the picture, flashing here and there upon a metal helmet or glinting upon the medals ..." It all amounted, declared *The Daily Telegraph & Courier*, to "a spectacle within a spectacle, a picture within a picture, a splendid tableau first and then an unrivalled panorama that rolled into multi-coloured and jewelled length round the grey, sun-beaten walls of the towering medieval fortress..."

Minute guns accompanied the procession as it wound its way up the castle to St. George's Chapel. The nine monarchs and King George V's two eldest sons followed on foot.

At Windsor Castle, the spectacle was no less impressive than what took place in London. Within the castle grounds itself, black-clad mourners watched in silence as the funeral cortege wound its way towards St. George's Chapel. Soldiers and sailors in their uniforms and clergy were present to pay homage. As the procession slowly wound its way through the Lower Ward, the wail of bagpipes played a mournful lament. "The skirl of the pipes and the whistle of the boatswains'" noted one report, "lent an eeriness to the ceremonial at Windsor that could be given by no other instruments."

Upon the gun-carriage's arrival at the foot of the stairs at the entrance to St. George's Chapel, the next, most important part of the funeral began – the religious service. Archbishops, bishops, other clergy, and court officials and heralds awaited the arrival of the coffin. As funeral marches were played on the chapel's organ, Grenadier Guards carried the royal coffin into the chapel. The *Office for the Burial of the Dead* was begun by the choir as the procession proceeded up the nave. Just behind the coffin walked King George V and Queen Alexandra, followed by the German Emperor with Queen Mary. Then came the Duke of Connaught with the other reigning sovereigns, then Prince Edward and Prince Albert, and the representatives of various nations, including Theodore Roosevelt.

It was fitting that King Edward VII was accorded his final resting place at St. George's Chapel. For it was within the Gothic edifice with its stained-glass windows and vaulted ceilings that the late King had been christened in 1842, and it was at St. George's where he had married Princess Alexandra of Denmark in 1863.

In the early afternoon of King Edward VII's funeral, sunlight flooded into the interior of St. George's Chapel, scattering about sparks of bright blue, red, and yellow from the stained-glass windows. The scent of flowers permeated from the wreaths given by mourners from all walks of life. Wreaths, elaborate and simple alike, had filled the Chapel and the adjoining cloister to overflowing. More wreaths were laid on the green velvety grass in front of the Chapel and propped against its walls. All in all, they totaled in the tens of thousands. "Parma violets and Madonna lilies," abounded along with "purple orchids and glorious yellow roses, cushions and crosses, and crowns and harps, and victor's wreaths of palms and laurels – it seemed as if all the conservatories of the land had been picked over by loving hands to find the choicest blooms out of which to fashion a wreath of sorrow for the dead King."

An eyewitness noted that "the service proceeded in an atmosphere which one felt to be charged with the deepest emotion." The scenes in St. George's were striking: "The splendour of the uniforms, the heraldic pomp, the dignity of the music, and above all, the beauty of the setting united to form a picture of unequalled beauty."

After the Archbishop of Canterbury read prayers, the Garter Principal King of Arms pronounced:

> *Thus it hath pleased the Almighty*
> *God to take out of this transitory life unto*

His Divine mercy, the late Most High, Most Mighty, and Most Excellent Monarch, Edward VII, by the Grace of God of the United Kingdom of Great Britain and Ireland, and of the British Dominions beyond the Seas, King, Defender of the Faith, Emperor of India, and Sovereign of the Most Noble Order of the Garter.

A hymn followed and then a solemn rendition of the national anthem was played in which all stood at attention. The Archbishop of Canterbury pronounced a benediction, silence followed, and the service ended. "The Kings passed one by one," noted an eyewitness, "none more noticeable than the youthful figures of King Alfonso and King Manuel, both of whom loved the late King Edward, while to both he gave generously of his great experience."

In writing of the funeral to her son, Tsar Nicholas II, the Dowager Empress Marie Feodorovna of Russia told him how it had been "the saddest and hardest day of all." It was also exhausting. Having left Buckingham Palace at nine in the morning, the Dowager Empress wrote to Nicholas, saying that it, "took three hours to drive to the station [Paddington], were at Windsor at 1 p.m. and came back here [London] at six." Everything went off well. "It was all beautifully arranged, all in perfect order, very touching and solemn." As for her sister, the newly widowed Queen, and her nephew, the new King, Marie Feodorovna noted: "Poor Aunt Alix bore up wonderfully to the last. Georgie, too, behaved so well and with such calm. But it is so unspeakably sad here now, his [Edward VII] absence is so deeply felt everywhere."

In his reply to his mother, Tsar Nicholas wrote: "By following the events in the English newspapers I was able to imagine the atmosphere of the funeral ceremonies and to feel what you must have gone through."

It was indeed trying for the Dowager Empress of Russia to participate in the obsequies for her departed brother-in-law, King Edward VII. But it had been trying day as well for George V. For the King had a "hatred of funerals and memorial services" and so to have had to bury his father to whom George V had been close, could not have been easy for the new British monarch.

King George V was host at Windsor to his fellow visiting monarchs; and to commemorate the unprecedented gathering, an official photograph was taken. The group, still resplendent in their military uniforms gathered in a corner of the White Drawing Room at Windsor Castle. Beneath a portrait of King Edward VII's father, the Prince Consort, the various monarchs presented a united front. In front sat Britain's King George V, flanked by Spain's King Alfonso XIII and Denmark's King Frederick VIII. Standing behind them were King Haakon VII of Norway, Tsar Ferdinand I of Bulgaria, King Manuel II of Portugal, Germany's Kaiser Wilhelm II, King George I of the Hellenes, and King Albert I of the Belgians.

Sir Frederick Ponsonby, who was among those responsible for arranging the final ceremonies at Windsor Castle, recorded that, "the gathering of Kings at Windsor was truly remarkable..." Of the impressive presence of sovereigns, Ponsonby recalled that "of these [monarchs] by far the greatest personalities were the German Emperor and the King of Bulgaria." Ponsonby had harsh words about Tsar Ferdinand I, whom he thought "had a strong but evil personality." In contrast, the King of Spain was "perhaps the cleverest of them, but the nicest to meet was the King of Norway."

King Haakon VII of Norway at 6 foot 3 inches was the tallest of the group. The eldest were the brother-kings, George I of the Hellenes and Frederick VIII of Denmark, along with Tsar Ferdinand I of Bulgaria. The middle-aged ones were the German Emperor and King George V. Those who still exuded youth but were easing into their middling years were Belgium's and Norway's monarchs. By far the youngest in appearance, age, and demeanor were the Iberian Kings: Alfonso XIII and Manuel II.

On the day that this historic photograph was taken, no one knew what was in store for these monarchs. It was still the heyday of kings, though rumbles of trouble on the political front had occasionally made themselves heard. Still, a cataclysmic war, let alone the jarring end of dynasties was far from many minds.

The relative peace that pervaded King Edward VII's reign, in contrast with the tragedies and great upheavals wrought by World War I just a few years later, contributed to a perception of the Edwardian Era as an age where uninterrupted peace and tranquility prevailed. But the era was not completely the golden age it had been made out to be where it was thought to be a decade solely of "calm and contentment, of pomp and luxury, of assured wealth and unchallenged order." In fact, "court splendours apart, it was none of those things. It was an era of growth and strain, of idealism and reaction, of swelling changes and of seething unrest." In Britain, "politics had never been so bitter; and abroad, the clouds were massing for Armageddon." Such were the words of one historian who wrote of the era some twenty plus years after its passing. But for those who witnessed that somber yet spectacular funeral of King Edward VII on May 20, 1910, whether at London or Windsor, a sense of pride, glory, and exultation in Britain, the late King, in Empire, and in royalty had to have passed the minds of a good number of the 2 million plus mourners.

The impressive and unparalleled funeral of King Edward VII – an apotheosis of sorts - no doubt sealed the King's reign in a golden haze of splendor. The magnificent obsequies helped cement the Edward Era in some minds as a seemingly permanent way of life. King and Empire were firmly ensconced. It was the triumph of royalty; and the procession of nine reigning kings during the funeral cortege appeared to underscore this. But unbeknownst to those who witnessed the spectacle, it was to be one of the last great moments of royal splendor. In just four years, Europe would be convulsed in war; and by 1918, three of the monarchs present at King Edward's funeral would be forced to vacate their thrones and one would be one felled by an assassin. Europe would never be the same again as on that bright, warm May day in 1910 when a pageant of kings paid homage to one of their own.

.

Chapter 3. King Manuel II of Portugal (1889-1932)

(reigned 1908-1910)

King Manuel II of Portugal, c. 1910

W hat then, became of those nine reigning sovereigns who rode in such splendor in London to pay homage to King Edward VII? The following pages tell a brief story of each monarch and what ultimately became of him and his throne. The first of the kings is Manuel II of Portugal who was the youngest of the nine reigning monarchs – he was just twenty when he attended the funeral of King Edward VII. Of the four monarchs who lost their thrones, Manuel II was also the first of the four to fall. What made Manuel II unique among his fellow monarchs was the dramatic manner in which he ascended the Portuguese throne.

****

King Manuel II of Portugal was born on November 15, 1889 in Lisbon, the third child and second son of King Carlos I of Portugal and his wife, Princess Amélie of Orléans. Through his mother, King Manuel was a great-great grandson of Louis Philippe I, King of the French. In appearance, Manuel resembled neither his father nor older brother, with their blond hair and tendency to corpulence. Instead, Manuel took after his mother, with her dark hair and dark eyes. Manuel had an uneventful childhood dominated by the usual rigors of the classroom. His mother's influence was strong; she had taught young Manuel to a large degree. One contemporary publication described Manuel as having been "brought up under the eye of his mother, who never expected to see him on the throne and who gave him a pious and even severe training." Part of Prince Manuel's education involved him serving as a midshipman in Portugal's navy. Manuel grew to enjoy sports and was good at shooting, skittles, billiards, and tennis. He also rode well and became adept at shoeing horses "which he learned to please his mother," who was the "best horsewoman in the whole [Iberian] peninsula." Manuel, it was said, also had "made it his business to shoe her Majesty's favorite steed himself."

Portugal's monarchy stretched back to the 12th century and the House of Braganza, to which Manuel belonged, had ruled Portugal since the 17th century. This lengthy hold on the throne by the Braganzas did not help Prince Manuel's family when it came to maintaining their popularity. Moreover, political instability contributed to rising tensions in Portugal during the latter years of Carlos I's reign. By 1906, the Cortes, or parliament, became "an assembly of obstruction and disorder" and "the small Republican contingency made the best possible use of the dissension within the political system to attack the monarchical regime."

On February 1, 1908, King Carlos I and Queen Amélie, and their sons, Crown Prince Luis and Prince Manuel, were riding in an open carriage in Lisbon when several revolutionaries fired a barrage of bullets at the royal family. King Carlos died instantly and his heir, Prince Luis, died minutes later. Manuel was also shot in the arm, face, and side, but survived. Queen Amélie bravely tried to fight off one of the assassins by hitting him with her bouquet of flowers. But within several minutes, she had tragically lost her husband and elder son in a notorious regicide that made her second son, Manuel, King of Portugal. The double murders of the King and his heir shocked Europe and garnered sympathy not only for the widowed Queen Amélie, but also for her only surviving child, the new King, Manuel II, who at his accession, became the youngest monarch in Europe.

In London, King Edward VII and Queen Alexandra, accompanied by their son and daughter-in-law, the Prince and Princess of Wales, cabinet ministers, and foreign ambassadors, attended a Requiem Mass at St. James's Church for the souls of the dead royals. King Edward VII's presence at a Roman Catholic Mass caused consternation among a number of stringent Protestants. This stemmed from the fact that the British King was titular head of the Church of England. Nevertheless, King

Edward VII ignored the strenuous objections such as those that emanated from the Protest Alliance.

King Edward and Queen Alexandra's son, the future King George V, was shaken, also, by the double assassinations. "Too horrible," was how George described it, adding that, "Portugal has been a disturbed State for some time."

Back in Lisbon, the funeral for King Carlos and his son was a somber affair. However, the shocking murders had not garnered sympathy from a number of the late King's subjects. One major British periodical that covered the funeral told its readers that there were numerous "apathetic spectators" in the streets and as evidence of this, "few heads [were] uncovered as the hearses passed." Such apathy from his people boded ill for the young King Manuel. The heavy pall of threatened assassination also hovered over the young King. Rumors were rampant that Manuel would be killed when he opened his first Parliament; and the Republican press churned out dire warnings telling Manuel II not to forget the fate of King Carlos I.

Manuel II was acclaimed King of Portugal in Lisbon's Chamber of Deputies in what was described by a contemporary publication as a "brilliant ceremony." The "boy king" as Manuel was described, conducted himself with dignity. At the throne, Manuel, draped in a velvet and ermine cloak, was handed the royal scepter. After Manuel gave a short address to parliament, the royal standard was unfurled and shouts of "vivas from the whole assembly" portended a successful and long reign. This echoed the sentiments of one British publication which had noted that despite the tragic circumstances surrounding Manuel II's accession, its readers were told that: "As a good omen it is recalled that the reign of Manuel I (1495-1521) was prosperous."

Throughout his short reign, King Manuel II elicited feelings of both disdain and approval. Despite signs of indifference on the streets of Lisbon to the new monarch during the funerals of his brother and father, a year-and-a-half after his accession, Manuel II had become a sympathetic figure with a number of his subjects. A British newspaper correspondent stationed in Lisbon noted that in 1909 many Portuguese "of all classes" were "well disposed towards the young monarch." No doubt Manuel II's "noble bearing, his kindly word and acts, and his stern devotion to duty and his country's good" contributed to this feeling of goodwill. Nevertheless, this reporter also noted ominously that Lisbon was in ferment, for "it may be doubted whether there is any revolutionary centre in Europe except in Barcelona and St.

Petersburg more restless than Lisbon." The Portuguese capital was nothing short of a "turbulent city."

In the fall of 1909, King Manuel paid an official state visit to England where he was received by King Edward VII. Edward invested young Manuel – who turned twenty during his visit – with England's oldest order of chivalry, the Order of the Garter, in a ceremony rich in pomp at Windsor Castle. There had been some talk of King Manuel, who adhered to a foreign policy that continued Portugal's long alliance with Britain, might come to marry a British princess, a project King Edward VII promoted. After all, Manuel II's counterpart on the Iberian Peninsula, King Alfonso XIII of Spain, had done just that in 1906 when he married a niece of King Edward VII. It was thought that King Manuel, who was the most eligible bachelor in Europe at the time of his visit, might become engaged to King Edward VII's granddaughter, Princess Alexandra of Fife, who had been staying at Windsor Castle at the same time as the Portuguese King, but the young Princess and King did not form an attachment for each other. In the end, King Manuel did not marry a British princess, like his Spanish counterpart.

Because the murders of King Manuel's father and brother were still fresh in many minds, his visit to Windsor Castle was marked by "extraordinary precautions" when it came to his security. In a contemporary account of this visit, Scotland's *St. Andrews Citizen*, told its readers in describing King Manuel II: "… we know that despite his bright face and merry smile his bright uniform must cover a heavy heart." King Manuel did, indeed, have a heavy heart, for he could never shake off the horrible killings of his father and brother, which occurred in his presence. "Nobody in this world can have an idea or even imagine what it was like!" King Manuel once wrote of the regicide. "I believe that only my poor, beloved mother and I really know…" And in recalling his murdered father and brother, Manuel added, "My God, how I miss them!"

Manuel II did not have the consolation of enjoying a stable, long reign. After his state visit to England, instability quickly took hold in Portugal where quarrels between political parties grew increasingly virulent. Moreover, disunity among the pro-monarchist parties in contrast to the strengthening of the pro-Republicans soon cast a shadow. Revolutionaries gained the upper hand at the expense of the moderates. Pro-republican propaganda began to make headway with the Portuguese people. Social and political unrest grew so that by 1910, the political landscape of Portugal took on an increasingly anti-monarchical hue. Such was the case in May 1910 when Manuel II left for London to attend the funeral of King Edward VII. King Manuel, who was still only twenty at the time, looked his age; and anyone who caught a glimpse of the sovereigns during the funeral processions, and Manuel II in particular, would have been in no doubt that he was the most junior of all his fellow monarchs.

Upon his return home, Manuel II faced a Portugal that continued to be wracked by political instability. The King's friendship with a French dancer, Gaby Deslys, provided anti-monarchical propaganda. In October 1910, the Portuguese army did not quell a mutiny on warships anchored on the Tagus River in Lisbon. Determined to make a stand, King Manuel returned to Lisbon to face the troubles. At first, King Manuel wanted to join the troops loyal to him and lead them in their fight against their enemies. But when the rebellious crews onboard the naval ships in Lisbon began shelling the royal palace, endangering those there, Manuel II's advisers counseled him to proceed to Oporto, to which he agreed, still determined not to leave Portugal. But further advice from councilors urged the King to leave the country, a move to which he reluctantly agreed. From Portugal, Manuel and his mother fled to Gibraltar. From there, the former Queen Amélie received a telegram addressed to her from Britain's King George V: "Manuel will have told you how distressed I have been and how deeply I have felt for you during this terrible time I am so glad you are coming to England and that I am able to place my yacht at your disposal [Queen] Mary and I send you our best love." And so it was on the British royal yacht, the *Victoria and Albert*, that Manuel fled to England where he was met by King George V. It was not surprising that King Manuel sought refuge in England. His mother was born in Twickenham and lived in England prior to becoming Portugal's Queen and had been a close friend of Britain's royal family.

Writing to her son, Tsar Nicholas II, the Dowager Empress Marie of Russia expressed her sorrow and indignation at events in Portugal:

> *The unfortunate young King, his mother and grandmother, it hurts one even to think of what they had to go through ... What a sad fate for this poor family, already so sorely tried! ... What a nasty mess in Portugal! How one hates having to recognise a republic there – we* [i.e., Russia] *are not going to till everybody else has, and then as late as possible.*

Others were not as sympathetic as the Dowager Empress of Russia had been on the fate of

King Manuel. *Harper's Weekly* informed their readers that:

> *The collapse of the Portuguese monarchy ... occasioned small surprise to those who had followed political affairs in that tiny kingdom. The throne went down under the dead weight of corruption and extravagance, which had alienated all elements, so that King Manuel reigned unfriended and unsupported, and the Republicans had the choosing of their own time and opportunity*
>
> .

Ultimately, as one scholar has concluded:

> *Revolution swept the Braganzas from their throne in October 1910 because of a combination of factors: financial, political, and religious. Yet at the heart of the revolution was the unescapable truth that an inexperienced young monarch placed his faith in outdated institutions and pusillanimous advisors. Under such circumstances, the House of Braganza failed to justify its existence, so it ceased to rule over an ancient kingdom.*

Though he had lost his throne, Manuel was fortunate in that neither he nor his family were executed. Exile was their fate. The overthrow of the monarchy had not embittered the former King of

Portugal but months after the event, Manuel still had not let go of the concept that he was no longer a reigning monarch. Such were his sentiments when Manuel met in 1911 with Winston Churchill, the future British Prime Minister who was then Home Secretary. Manuel begun their talk by telling Churchill that, "I am a King and it is as a King that I must manage my affairs." At that same meeting the former monarch had impressed the future British Prime Minister. Churchill told his wife in a letter that he found Manuel to have been religiously "devout" and "intelligent." He was also a very "charming boy – Full of gravity & conviction, & yet in spite of his sorry plight – a boy full of life & spirits." One of Manuel's friends, Prince Christopher of Greece, echoed Churchill's observation, describing Manuel as "having a schoolboy's love of fun." Moreover "he was deeply religious" and "was a brilliant musician … one of the best amateur pianists" Prince Christopher had ever heard.

In September 1913, the former King of Portugal married Princess Augusta Victoria of Hohenzollern and together, the couple set up home at Fulwell Park, near Twickenham. Surrounding the Georgian-style mansion were twenty-two acres of lawns and gardens. The River Crane flowed through the grounds of Fulwell Park, affording the couple the chance to row and fish on the river.

With the outbreak of World War I, Manuel wanted to contribute to the war effort and serve in the British Army and fight for France (as his mother had been a French princess). The British government, however, denied this request. Manuel then chose to be of help by looking after servicemen who had been wounded and took an active role in supporting the British Red Cross. In November 1915, Manuel wrote to his mother from France where he had visited injured Allied soldiers:

> *It has been impossible for me to write to you these days ... I have not stopped for a moment ... what horrors you see! I attended two operations ... in 2 days I visited 12 hospitals ... and I spoke to 500 officers and soldiers...*

Manuel continued to follow events in Portugal and was full of concern in 1915, when the former monarch wrote, "the international situation in Portugal is simply heartbreaking, because unfortunately no one takes us seriously."

Besides the enormous loss of life and social upheaval wrought by World War I, the conflict also contributed to the downfall of more monarchies. When Tsar Nicholas II of Russia abdicated in 1917 after revolution had swept through his capital, Manuel wrote to King George V about "these terrible events in Russia! I know unhappily by my own experience what a revolution is & I can understand it better than anybody else." The memories were still raw for Manuel who added, "I feel very much upset & sorry: upset by what a revolution means, sorry because I am very fond of poor Nicky…"

Four years into the Great War, Manuel was full of patriotic fervor for the land where he resided, telling King George V: "We just returned now from church where we have been praying God, to protect the British Army & Navy, to bless their King & to give us soon the complete victory!" Manuel still had not lost his strong desire to fight for England, adding that: "You know too well my dear Georgie that my ambition would be to be fighting & that my service could be more useful either at the front or here in England my adopted country."

Manuel and his wife continued to live in his adopted country where he kept busy acquiring and cataloguing in great scholarly detail a library of rare early Portuguese books. From Fulwell Park, Manuel wrote of his endeavor, saying that he "was preparing the publication of his catalogue, from 1489 to 1600, with about 700 reproductions; it will be an interesting work and that I deem useful, since it was never done in this way." Manuel also took an active interest in the area he lived in. Manuel and his wife worshiped at Twickenham's St. James Roman Catholic Church, becoming benefactors of the church. Manuel also supported local events and causes. In 1927, the former King of Portugal had won 16 prizes and two cups at a flower and vegetable show in Twickenham.

Hopes for a restoration of the Portuguese monarchy faded with the years. After World War I, there was a spark of hope when in 1919, the monarchical movement in Portugal seemed to have gained ground when a Royalist Government had been reportedly formed in Oporto. However, nothing came of this and Manuel never came close to regaining his throne.

The former King nevertheless always kept abreast of what went on in Portugal, writing to a friend in 1926 that, "I always try to serve my Country..." That year, a military coup had brought an end to the unstable First Portuguese Republic. "May God have mercy on Portugal!" wrote Manuel, who, despite having been exiled from his country for many years, could never stop thinking of his native land. Manuel died unexpectedly of a sudden edema of the throat on July 2, 1932 at Fulwell Park after complaining of pains in his throat. Manuel was only forty-three. He left no heirs as he and his wife had been childless.

The tragic circumstances of his accession to the Portuguese throne in 1908 when Manuel was still a teenager contributed in no small measure to his eventual overthrow two short years later. "Handicapped by both his youth and lack of training for the duties" of his role as king led to Manuel II's downfall. The assassination of Manuel's father meant that "the Portuguese monarchy had effectively expired with King Carlos, for Manuel was not an heir but an orphan." In the end, unlike his namesake, King Manuel I, who was dubbed "the Fortunate" because his reign had occurred during the golden age of Portuguese overseas discovery and conquest in the early sixteenth century, King Manuel II, because of the double assassinations of his father and brother and his own brief, unstable reign that ended in a life of exile, earned the moniker, "the Unfortunate."

Chapter 4. King Frederick VIII
of Denmark (1843-1912)
(reigned 1906-1912)

King Frederick VIII of Denmark, c. 1909

Like his brother, King George I of the Hellenes, Denmark's King Frederick VIII was the son a king (Christian IX of Denmark), brother to a queen (Alexandra of the

United Kingdom) and an empress (Marie
Feodorovna of Russia), brother-in-law of a king
(Edward VII of the United Kingdom), and uncle to
an emperor (Nicholas II of Russia). Frederick VIII
was also the father of two kings (Christian X of
Denmark and Haakon VII of Norway). Frederick
VIII of Denmark reigned for only six short years,
from 1906 to 1912. Like his brother-in-law,
Britain's King Edward VII, Frederick VIII
ascended the throne at a late age, in his case, at the
age of sixty-two. Of the nine kings present at King
Edward VII's funeral only King Frederick VIII and
his brother, King George I of Greece, did not live to
see World War I.

****

The future King Frederick VIII of Denmark
was born on June 3, 1843, the son of Prince
Christian of Schleswig-Holstein-Sonderburg-
Glücksburg and his wife, Princess Louise of Hesse-
Kassel. Frederick was the eldest child in a family of
three boys and three girls. During Prince
Frederick's early years there was little indication of
the spectacular good fortune that would come to his
family. Things began to change when in 1853,
Frederick's father became Prince of Denmark and
heir to the Danish throne. In 1860, Prince

Frederick, along with his sister, Princess Alexandra, were confirmed in the Lutheran faith. This event marked the end of the Prince's childhood and the beginning of his adulthood. Like his siblings, Prince Frederick grew up to be "tall and distinguished-looking."

Prince Frederick, along with his younger brother, Prince William, were both enrolled as cadets at the Danish Naval Academy. Frederick was a popular figure with his comrades as was his brother, William. Prince Frederick's future was already mapped out for him as he was destined to be Denmark's next king after his father. But in a curious twist of fate, his younger brother, Prince William, became Greece's new monarch when he was chosen to be King of the Hellenes in 1863. Prince William, who became King George I of the Hellenes, left for Greece and his new kingdom, at the young age of seventeen.

The year 1863 had been a momentous one for Prince Frederick's family. Not only had his brother, William, become Greece's King George I, their sister, Alexandra, became Princess of Wales when she married Queen Victoria's eldest son and heir, the future King Edward VII. At the end of the year, Frederick's father became King Christian IX of Denmark, making Frederick at the age of nineteen, Crown Prince of Denmark. His family's spectacular rise thus became evident in 1863. The family's luster burned even brighter when Prince Frederick's sister, Dagmar, married in 1866, the future Tsar Alexander III of Russia.

If 1863 was a year of good fortune for the Danish royal family, 1864 proved the opposite. That year Prussia and Austria declared war on Denmark. Prince Frederick served in the war on Denmark's side. In the end, Denmark lost the war and its territories of Schleswig-Holstein, indelibly creating a strong anti-German sentiment within Frederick's own family.

With Frederick's sisters, Alexandra and Dagmar, having made such illustrious marriages to the British and Russian heirs to the throne, Frederick's mother had hoped that he could make an equally advantageous marriage. He was sent to study at Oxford University and while in England, Crown Prince Frederick had hoped to marry one of Queen Victoria's daughters. But the Queen would have none of it. With this plan dashed, Prince Frederick married in 1869 Princess Louisa of Sweden-Norway. Princess Louisa had the prerequisite pedigree needed in a future consort but lacked looks which she more than made up for with her wealth. Crown Prince Frederick and his siblings were noted for their good looks, but financially, they were much more impoverished than other royals. Princess Louisa, with her wealth, was thus a welcome addition to the Danish royals. Prince Frederick's wife was known in the family as 'the Swan' and 'Aunt Swan' to younger members. An extremely religious woman who rarely ventured into society, 'Aunt Swan,' remarked England's future Queen Mary in 1896, was "a good soul but a little queer in the head & very difficult to get along with as she is so stiff." In time, Frederick and Louisa became the parents of eight children, two of whom became kings; one of Denmark and the other of Norway.

Because Crown Prince Frederick's father, King Christian IX, had numerous descendants who belonged to the royal houses of Denmark, England, Russia, and Greece, it was not uncommon to find large family gatherings being hosted in Denmark by the Danish royals. Prince Frederick's brothers-in-law, the future King Edward VII and Tsar Alexander III of Russia dutifully attended these family gatherings. Frederick's Russian brother-in-law thoroughly enjoyed the practical jokes and easy informality that permeated the Danish royal family, a sentiment not shared by Frederick's British brother-in-law, Edward.

The close relations the Danish royal family enjoyed with the British royal family through the marriage of Crown Prince Frederick's sister,

Princess Alexandra, to the Prince of Wales, was cemented even further in 1893 when Frederick's second son, Prince Carl, married Princess Alexandra's youngest daughter, Princess Maud of Wales. At the time of the marriage, it was assumed that Prince Carl would go on to pursue a career in the Danish Navy. All that changed in 1905 when the union of Sweden and Norway was dissolved and in the process Prince Carl was chosen as a candidate for the new crown of Norway.

In 1905, Crown Prince Frederick became active in the political discussions concerning the candidature for the new Norwegian throne. King Edward VII was even more adamant about Prince Carl's candidature. The King advised his son-in-law to waste no time in accepting the offer of the Norwegian crown, lest Kaiser Wilhelm II of Germany make trouble and scuttle Carl's candidacy. King Edward urged Carl to "pray warn your Grandfather and Father when the German Emperor comes to be firm." As for Crown Prince Frederick, he did not press his son's candidature until it was certain that King Oscar of Sweden would relinquish his title as King of Norway, which he eventually did. Finally, in November 1905, Prince Carl became King Haakon VII of Norway.

In 1906, Crown Prince Frederick and his wife attended the enthronement of their son, Haakon

VII, as King of Norway at Nidaros Cathedral in Trondheim. At this point, Frederick had seen his father become King of Denmark, his brother become King of Greece, a sister become Queen of England, another sister become Empress of Russia, a nephew become Tsar of Russia; and now his own son was King of Norway. Frederick's turn at becoming a monarch finally arrived when his father, King Christian IX, died in January 1906. One periodical noted that the new King's "liberal tendencies caused him at times to be in conflict with his father, but his opinions never disturbed the harmony of the relations existing between himself and the late King Christian." Frederick, who had been Crown Prince of Denmark for some forty-three years, assumed the throne as King Frederick VIII. The new Danish monarch, who was sixty-two years old at his accession, took as his motto, 'The Lord be my helper.' Frederick VIII was attached to his countrymen, and his energies "were devoted with singleness of aim to promoting the welfare of his kingdom."

King Frederick VIII did not distinguish himself as a consummate diplomatist like King Edward VII, nor was he bombastic like Kaiser Wilhelm II. Frederick did not possess the deviousness and unscrupulousness of Tsar Ferdinand I of Bulgaria; nor did he possess the shrewdness of his brother,

King George I of Greece nor the excellent attention to duty that Britain's George V had. Frederick VIII not display the courage King Albert of the Belgians nor did Frederick have the spirited personality of the Iberian monarchs, King Manuel II of Portugal and King Alfonso XIII of Spain. In fact, King Frederick was largely overshadowed by his fellow monarchs; and as one British periodical put it, "the personality of the King remained comparatively unknown to the European public." And if one British courtier is to be believed, King Frederick simply did not impress. While attending an official banquet in Copenhagen, this courtier, King Edward VII's Assistant Private Secretary, Sir Frederick Ponsonby, noted that as he listened to King Frederick replying to a speech given by King Edward VII, the following impression emerged:

> *At first, I thought he was speaking Danish as I could not understand a word, but later on I grasped the fact that he was speaking in English. He was a man who was most anxious to please everybody. At first he thought it would be popular to throw in his lot with the extreme Left, but finding that this antagonized the landowners, he veered round and ended by pleasing no one. He seemed to have little personality and few brains.*

King Frederick VIII tried to be a successful monarch for Denmark. He also wanted to be well-liked and to this end, according to one commentator, the King, "anxious for popularity," had been "quite willing to don the cap of liberty and promise anything to his people."

Unlike his sister, Queen Alexandra, and her husband, King Edward VII, who reigned over a country that was a European Power, Frederick VIII reigned over a small, much weaker kingdom. He could not assert himself against neighboring Germany and its Kaiser as King Edward VII could. Because of this, Frederick VIII sought better relations with Germany. Frederick VIII made an official visit to Kaiser Wilhelm II in Berlin, hoping that he could secure for Danes living in German-controlled Schleswig, better rights. King Frederick also visited Iceland, which was part of Denmark, and advocated for Iceland's greater independence.

When it came to Danish journalists, King Frederick VIII enjoyed sparring with them, earning him the moniker of the "editor's terror." The King invited editors to his palace to discuss the political issues of the day. Once the invited editor gave his opinions or views, the King would then go to a nearby bookshelf and "taking down a large scrapbook," Frederick VIII would "gravely" proceed "to read the printed leaders of some previous issue of the editor's journal, probably expressing diametrically opposite views."

King Frederick VIII, in common with his fellow Scandinavian monarchs, was not interested in associating the monarchy with much pomp and ceremony. In fact, the King had a liking for maintaining a degree of anonymity. "He had," as one publication put it, "no love for notoriety." This penchant for anonymity was evident when a group of tourists, not recognizing the King, asked him if they may see the royal gardens. "Certainly," replied Frederick VIII. "Come with me and I will show you over them," he added. Upon taking leave of his guests, Frederick VIII casually remarked: "If you would like to see the Royal stables also, just say you have the King's permission."

Having ascended the throne at the mature age of sixty-two, King Frederick VIII could not enjoy a long reign like his father before him. As it turned out, Frederick VIII only reigned for six years. On May 14, 1912, the King with some members of his family, had stopped at Hamburg, Germany on the way back to Denmark from the French Riviera where he had been convalescing from ill health. While in Hamburg, King Frederick chose to stay at his hotel incognito. At one point, the King went out for a walk, unattended. Not far from his hotel, the King felt dizzy and staggered. A policeman saw him and came to his aid. The King had suffered a heart attack and soon died. King Frederick carried no identification with him and consequently his body was placed in the city mortuary along with other unidentified ones. By the evening, a frantic search by the King's attendants ensued. Only early the next morning did the family learn that the body of an unidentified man lay in the city's morgue. The body turned out to be that of the late King.

The circumstances of King Frederick VIII of Denmark's death were described in poignant terms to the readers of one British newspaper: "To the superficial observer there may seem something strange in this termination of a King's career. They may see in the laying of his dead body side by side in a public mortuary with the 'common clay' of the meaner people a touch of the irony of fate and the democracy of death…"

In writing of the sad news, England's Queen Mary noted of her late uncle: "The sad news of poor U. Freddy's death … came as a great shock to us all as we had heard he was better." "It is all very sad," the Queen added, "and his dying in the street quite alone makes it worse…" King Frederick VIII's body was brought back for burial in Denmark. He was succeeded by his son, King Christian   X.

Chapter 5. King George I of Greece (1845-1913)

(reigned 1863-1913)

H.M. KING OF GREECE

King George I of Greece

O f the nine kings who attended the funeral of King Edward VII, King George I of the Hellenes (of the Greeks) had one of the most tragic endings, for he was felled by an assassin's bullet in 1913. Himself a king, George I was the father of a king (Constantine I of Greece), and also had the distinction of being the son of a king (Christian IX of Denmark); the brother of another (King Frederick VIII of Denmark), a queen (Alexandra of the United Kingdom) and an empress (Marie Feodorovna of Russia); as well as being uncle to four kings (Haakon VII of Norway, Christian X of Denmark, Constantine I of Greece, and George V of the United Kingdom) and an emperor (Tsar Nicholas II of Russia). King George I's sister, Queen Alexandra, was married to King Edward VII, thus making George the brother-in-law to the British monarch whose funeral he attended in 1910.

****

King George I was born Prince William of Schleswig-Holstein-Sonderburg-Glucksburg in 1845 at Copenhagen, Denmark, the second son of Prince Christian of Schleswig-Holstein-Sonderburg-Glucksburg and his wife, Princess Louise of Hesse-Kassel. Prince William (known in the family as 'Willy'), along with his parents and three sisters and two brothers, lived in relatively moderate circumstances in the Danish capital. The family's fortunes, however, were soon on the rise. In 1863, Prince William's father ascended to the Danish throne as King Christian IX. That same year, Prince William's sister, Alexandra, married the Prince of Wales, Queen Victoria's eldest son and heir – the man who would become in 1901, Britain's King Edward VII. Then in 1866, Prince William's other sister, Princess Dagmar, married into the Russian imperial family when she wed the Tsarevich Alexander – the future Tsar Alexander III. The couple became the parents of the ill-fated Tsar Nicholas II.

Prince William himself had been a part of the Danish royal family's meteoric rise to significance. Only three weeks after his sister, Princess Alexandra, married the future King Edward VII, Willy was elected King of the Hellenes (of the Greeks) in March 1863 by the Greek National Assembly. Prince William had not been the first choice to become Greece's next king. Prince Alfred, Queen Victoria's second son was also in the running, but the Queen rejected the offer. And so, the mantle of kingship fell on Denmark's Prince William, whose candidature was supported by Britain. The seventeen-year-old Naval Academy student learned that he had been chosen as King of the Hellenes when Willy saw the article about his accession in a newspaper in which his lunch of a sandwich of sardines had been wrapped.

Prince William had been hesitant about accepting the offer of the Greek throne and said, "I should like to think it over for an hour..." The Danish Prince went into a garden and pondered what to do. There, William "fought out his battle all alone, gave up for ever the peace and security of Denmark, his cherished dream of the sea." When Prince William formally accepted the offer of the throne of Greece the next day, from a Greek deputation, the composed Prince "gave no sign of the effort the decision had cost him." It did not help young Willy that his father, Prince Christian, was opposed to his son becoming Greece's next king. To Prince Christian, the Greek throne amounted to "a crown of thorns." Prince Christian, therefore, sought reassurances from the European Powers for his son, and only after these were given did he reluctantly allow his son to assume the Greek crown. Upon his accession, William took the name of 'George,' becoming King George I of the Hellenes. To help bolster King George's position, Britain ceded the Ionian Islands to Greece in 1864. King George I's father became King Christian IX of Denmark two weeks after George arrived in his new kingdom.

The young King George was under no illusions as to the stability of the Greek throne and the challenges he faced concerning his newly adopted country. In 1862, the previous King of Greece, Otto, a Prince of Bavaria, had been deposed, having failed to resolve Greece's numerous problems. The young George I, therefore, knew that his task as King of the Hellenes would not be an easy one. But there was hope that the new King from far-away Denmark would do better than King Otto. The British diplomat, Sir Horace Rumbold, was present in Athens when King George was officially welcomed. Rumbold noted how "the Athenians, indeed all the Greeks, went wild with joy and excitement, and gave their new sovereign a truly enthusiastic welcome."

King George I wasted no time in transferring his loyalty to Greece and seeking what was best for his new countrymen. Years later, in chronicling his impressions of his father, Prince Nicholas of Greece wrote that, "although he loved Denmark, Greece always came first."

King George I grew into an intelligent and charming man who has been described by a friend as having a "predilection for plain talk and manners that never failed to make an impression." Moreover, King George's "handsome features radiated all the shrewdness and alert intelligence" of his mother, Queen Louise of Denmark. The King's "blue eyes, noted for their merry twinkle and keenness of expression, reflected his youthfulness and lurking sense of humor which to the last were the dominating points of his character."

George I soon set about establishing a dynasty and married in 1867 Grand Duchess Olga of Russia, who was only sixteen. The choice of Olga as his wife and queen was helped in large part to her Orthodox faith. It was deemed necessary that a Queen of the Hellenes should hold the same faith as that of their subjects. George I and Queen Olga became the parents of five sons and three daughters. One of their grandsons, Prince Philip of Greece, married the future Queen Elizabeth II of the United Kingdom in 1947.

As his own sons grew into adults, King George I, for all his easygoing ways, became somewhat distant from them. Like his sisters, Alexandra in England, and Marie Feodorovna in Russia, George could never quite accept the fact that his sons were grown men. As one chronicler of the Danish royals put it: "So enduringly youthful in both looks and tastes themselves, these sons and daughters of King Christian IX insisted on treating their own offspring as children long after they had matured." This mentality had affected how King George I viewed his other younger relations as well. To England's future King George V, Uncle Willy's nephew, Greece's monarch would address him in letters with the Danish endearments of "*gamle pølse*" or "*gamle sylte*" – meaning "my dear old sausage" and "my dear old pickled pork."

In his private life, King George I may have retained his Danish ways, but "in public he was all Greek. His country's problems, and its aspirations, were his." King George I worked hard at being Greece's monarch. One of his sons recalled that King George's "day was never shorter than ten hours and more likely to run into twelve or even twenty-four when there was any crisis to be faced." George also learned the Greek language, traveled about the country, and did not venture abroad for the first four years of his reign.

Greece during the early years of King George's reign was in a dire state. The extent of difficulties facing the young George I in his new kingdom can be seen in the following historical account of the nation's troubles:

> *The state and its attendant offices were essentially regarded as prizes to be captured by rival cliques of politicians, and it is scarcely surprising that as a consequence there was little sense of collective loyalty to, or trust in, the state and*

*its institutions ... The wheels of the Greek
political machine were oiled not only by the
lavish dispensation of favours but also by
open bribery, electoral manipulation and
fraud.*

One contemporary of King George I
summed up the sad state of affairs in Greece in the
early years of the King's reign by stating that:

> *Things were in such a state that in
> some departments the very machinery of
> government had come to a standstill; in
> others it worked haltingly, as though the
> wheels did not catch properly ... The courts
> of justice, paralysed by hopelessness, had
> ceased sitting, for all prison gates had been
> thrown open ... this state of disorganisation
> gave a fresh impetus to brigandage, taxes
> remained unpaid, and the treasury was
> empty.*

One of King George I's goals had been to see
to the progress of Greece. Ever since the country
had wrestled independence from the Ottoman
Empire in 1831, numerous challenges plagued the
country – challenges, both on the domestic and
international front which George had to tackle.
Financial weakness and poverty had dogged Greece
as did wars such as the 1897 Greco-Turkish War
over Crete.

The challenges of being a monarch of Greece dogged King George throughout his reign. Vicky, the Crown Princess of Prussia (the eldest daughter of England's Queen Victoria), wrote in 1870 to her mother that, "the thrones of Greece and Rumania seem to me the most wretched and unenviable of positions." Nearly thirty years later, Vicky (whose daughter by then had married King George I's eldest son and heir), told her mother, Queen Victoria, of the challenges again facing George I:

> *The King is in a very difficult position. He could do a great deal more than he does, if he were to exercise his prerogative and use the power he has with more energy to break with abuses and introduce reforms. On the other hand, the King, who is very clever, has often had la main heureuse* [a happy touch] *and often saved the situation when it was full of danger, by his tact and conciliatory restraint and by letting people have their own way. That policy is no doubt wise and good, but does not always suffice and at the present moment seems to me a misfortune.*

The year 1897 was especially explosive for Greece and King George. With Crete having a large Greek population, calls for the island's annexation grew loud in Athens. Turkey responded by declaring war on Greece. The Greeks did not fare well in the war; and King George pleaded with his sister, Alexandra, the Princess of Wales, for British help. King George I's thinking was that as his sister was Queen Victoria's daughter-in-law, Alexandra could plead his case to the British. Princess Alexandra "did a great deal, bombarding Queen Victoria with telegrams" pleading her beleaguered brother's cause. But it was to no avail. The Greeks suffered a humiliating defeat and the Greek royal family's safety was imperiled. Greece fell into a deplorable state, "the northern towns being crowded with refugees and violence rife in the streets of Athens." Public opinion eventually turned back in favor of King George I and the royal family in 1898 when the King and one of his daughters escaped an assassination attempt.

Sir James Rennell Rodd, who served with the British legation in Athens in the 1890s, noted the difficulties faced by King George I. Rodd recalled a conversation he had with George I, recording in his memoirs that: "His own position, the King said, grew more and more difficult. He was expected to drive a coach without holding the reins. Politicians of all colours seemed to aim at depriving the Sovereign of the powers which the constitution accorded him, and without an element of stability such as the crown should present the country could not go on."

Tried as he might, King George I could not always control the volatile world of Greek politics. Not surprisingly, the fortunes of the Greek royal family during his reign fluctuated wildly. The King's youngest son, Prince Christopher, summed it up succinctly when he noted of one particular volatile year: "We never knew which way the pendulum was going to swing; we could only sit and wait with our trunks packed."

Despite the volatile nature of Greek politics and his tenuous hold on the throne, King George liked representing Greece abroad and had a favorite saying: "I am my own Ambassador." A contemporary described the King as not merely being an "ornamental figurehead" for the small kingdom of Greece; stating that King George had "been a real factor in international politics." This same observer noted that that the French statesman, Georges Clemenceau, had "publicly declared that he never in all his experience came across an abler diplomat or a more persuasive speaker than the King of the Hellenes."

Greece was fortunate in having George I as a monarch, but the region's volatility meant that the potential for war always cast a long shadow – especially as the Ottoman Empire continued to weaken through the years. By 1911, it was evident that trouble was brewing in the Balkans and that Greece would soon likely be engulfed in some kind of conflict. King George I's sister, Queen Alexandra, sought to help her brother again by urging her son, King George V, to support Greece by stating: "Remember England put my brother there and are bound to keep him there."

War broke out in the Balkans the next year. This time, Greece was prepared. There was to be no repeat of the ignominious defeat of 1897. The Greek army was much better trained. It was almost inevitable that Greece went to war. For years, the country had been animated by the Megali Idea, an irredentist movement that gained much ground during King George I's reign. The Megali Idea, which dominated Greek domestic and international relations, sought to 'redeem' unliberated lands in the Ottoman Empire which had dominant Greek populations. To this end, during the First Balkan War which began in 1912, Greece acquired Macedonia and Epirus.

King George I's greatest achievement occurred in November 1912 when Greek forces entered the port city of Salonika, just beating the Bulgarians to it. King George rode in triumph in the city to much acclaim, his forces having re-conquered from the Ottomans, Greek territory that had not been theirs for nearly five hundred years. "All his reign," recorded the King's son, Prince Nicholas, "he had dreamt of this supreme moment, which was such a glorious completion of his life's work." With such a great achievement, King George felt that his task had been completed. Greece, under his reign had practically doubled in size. The King had expressed his desire to abdicate in favor of his eldest son, after celebrating his Golden Jubilee, scheduled for the latter part of 1913. "I shall have reigned fifty years," said King George to his family, "it's enough for any king." Moreover, "I think I'm entitled to a little rest I my old age."

Fate, however, had other plans. The King, who disliked being shadowed by men trying to protect him from harm, went his way in public as much as possible without body guards protecting him. For King George I had "a deep-seated aversion to 'being shadowed like a murderer.'" This, combined with "his fondness for following the same route daily with the punctuality of a chronometer," proved fatal. On March 18, 1913, the King went for his usual afternoon walk in Salonika and was fatally shot by a Greek anarchist.

In assessing the reign of King George I of the Hellenes, one historian has concluded that: "George, by the standards of the time, and certainly in contrast to his predecessor and successor on the throne, had manifested a commitment to constitutional rule that had done much to inject an element of stability into Greek politics."

Sir James Rennell Rodd, who knew the King, summed up the life of George I when he wrote:

> *The Greek people owed a great debt to King George, who had handled many difficult situations with tact and adroitness. His family influences in the councils of Europe had often stood them in good stead. He had great personal charm and was deservedly popular in Athens, and not least so when he asserted himself. Had he travelled more often and more extensively in his dominions and made himself better known to his subjects in remoter provinces he would have been idolized, and might have exercised a still greater influence in public affairs. The Greek is democratic and monarchical at the same time, and feels a personal interest in his Sovereign. King George lived to see his little country grow into the greater Greece, and it was a dark day for all its well-wishers when the hand of an assassin at Salonika terminated his valuable life.*

Chapter 6. Tsar Ferdinand I of Bulgaria (1861-1948) (reigned 1887-1918)

Tsar Ferdinand of Bulgaria, c. 1912

W hen he attended the funeral of King Edward VII, Tsar Ferdinand of Bulgaria was generally referred to in the British media as 'King Ferdinand' although he assumed the title of 'Tsar' in 1908. Ferdinand was a dandy and the most flamboyant of Europe's monarchs. Kaiser Wilhelm, who himself liked to parade in grandiose military uniforms, once described Ferdinand I as being "festooned with decorations like a Christmas tree." But beneath this theatrical front lay a calculating mind. An arch-intriguer, Ferdinand's political machinations on behalf of his adopted kingdom earned him admirers and enemies alike.

****

Ferdinand I, Tsar of Bulgaria was a member of the House of Saxe-Coburg-Gotha and was born on February 26, 1861 in Vienna, the son of Prince Auguste of Saxe-Coburg-Gotha and his wife, Princess Clémentine of Orléans, a daughter of France's King Louis Philippe. A number of members of the Coburg dynasty had successfully ascended the thrones, or became consorts of reigning monarchs of countries such as Portugal, Belgium, and the United Kingdom (Prince Albert, husband of Queen Victoria was a Coburg). Ferdinand eventually added to that list, becoming in 1908, tsar or king.

Ferdinand may have been a Coburg on his paternal side, but he turned out to be "'his mother's son,' a Prince of the true Orleanist stamp." Princess Clémentine's keen ambitions helped propel Ferdinand to a more illustrious, albeit turbulent future than that of being an officer in the Austro-Hungarian army. Princess Clémentine, clever and intelligent, saw in her youngest child great potential and so "all her will, her energy and love were centered on her last born." In Ferdinand, Clémentine detected "natural gifts which might lead to the fulfilment of her ambition: to see her son crowned as king." In her son, Ferdinand, Princess Clémentine "felt she could foresee the full bloom of his inheritance – the brilliance of her French ancestors combined with the intellectual gifts of the Coburgs."

In time, the French Princess Clémentine's ambitions for her son and Prince Ferdinand's ambitions for himself focused on the Balkans. The gradual disintegration of the Ottoman Empire meant that the Balkans became a much-coveted area of Europe in which the Great Powers competed with each other for influence over the unstable region. After Russia's gains in the Russo-Turkish War of 1877-8, the Treaty of Berlin of 1878 signed by the Great Powers saw to the creation of the principality of Bulgaria. Prince Alexander of

Battenberg, a nephew of the Russian Tsar was duly elected Prince of Bulgaria in 1879. Russian interference in Bulgaria was strong; and in the end, Prince Alexander's aspirations for Bulgarian independence conflicted with Russia. A military coup by pro-Russian officers compelled Prince Alexander to abdicate in 1886. He left Bulgaria for a life of exile. Bulgaria went on the hunt again for another sovereign prince. The search culminated with the choice of Ferdinand of Saxe-Coburg-Gotha. In April 1887, the Crown Princess of Prussia wrote to her mother, Britain's Queen Victoria, about the rumors concerning Ferdinand:

> *We hear that it is a close secret, and that a Prince has been found ... the poor Bulgarians are in such straits that they will jump at a Prince who is in any degree eligible and then keep him. As Ferdinand is the first cousin of Minny (the Empress of Russia), it might be possible that he has been thought of ....*

Queen Victoria was not been disposed toward Prince Ferdinand. The Queen wrote in December 1886 of her opinions about the Prince: "Ferdinand proposed *himself*!! He is clever – but sickly very effeminate, a fop and not good-natured who would not remain there a year." Prince Ferdinand did not mind being seen as a fop. On the contrary, according to one contemporary aristocrat, Ferdinand "delighted" in being underestimated, feeling "that it was far more advantageous to pass for a fool than to be credited with an amount of intelligence one did not in reality possess."

Because the Great Powers did not formally recognize him as Prince of Bulgaria, Ferdinand had found himself from the outset in a delicate position. The Crown Princess of Prussia (who was an ardent supporter of the deposed Prince Alexander of Battenberg) wrote to her mother her thoughts on Prince Ferdinand: "The Bulgarians will soon realise that with the best intentions Ferdinand is not like their Hero Prince, to whom they behaved so badly and whom they must ever miss."

Time would tell whether Prince Ferdinand would prove himself more adept than Prince Alexander of Battenberg in navigating the treacherous waters of Bulgarian politics. The Russians, for one, continued to try and place Bulgaria under their sphere of influence. Moreover, war between Russia and the Ottoman Empire over the principality appeared inevitable. Though Bulgarian nationalism was proving a thorn to Russia, there was little doubt that Russia might try to dominate Ferdinand of Bulgaria as they had tried to do with Prince Alexander.

Ferdinand's acceptance of the Bulgarian throne was thus something of a poisoned chalice, owing to the instability of his newly adopted country. With the Ottoman Empire – the 'sick man of Europe' – declining and losing its hold on the Balkans, instability increased in the region. This in turn led to points of contention among the European Powers.

Bulgaria, with its highly-charged politics, nevertheless suited the ambitious Prince Ferdinand. Not content to be a mere figurehead, Ferdinand wanted to be a "strenuous king of men." A fledgling nation arising from the ashes of the disintegrating Ottoman Empire could offer Ferdinand much opportunity to exercise his ambitions; and so, it seemed obvious to him that, "a newly born nation in a state of anarchy required a second liberator, and the young Orleanist Prince felt confident in his ability" to be the monarch Bulgaria needed. Ferdinand accepted the offer of the Bulgarian throne with the following words:

> *I am both proud and grateful on account of the vote of the Great Assembly, which has elected me Prince of Bulgaria, and I hope to prove myself worthy of the confidence of the noble Bulgarian nation. I am ready to respond to the call of the Great Assembly which elected me with a unanimity*

which has deeply moved me, and through
them to the whole Bulgarian nation.

Upon arriving in Bulgaria, Ferdinand as sovereign Prince of Bulgaria promised to "consecrate my life to the happiness, greatness, and prosperity of my dear people."

In 1893 Prince Ferdinand married Princess Maria Luisa of Bourbon-Parma, the daughter of the last sovereign Duke of Parma. It was an arranged marriage and unhappy one. Nevertheless, the couple became the parents of four children, including the heir, Prince Boris. In 1908 the widowed Ferdinand married Princess Eleanore Reuss of Köstritz. Ferdinand had little affection for his wives. His main obsession centered on politics and achieving success for Bulgaria and his dynasty.

Ferdinand of Bulgaria was determined to shake off Ottoman suzerainty and sought Russian help and influence in his quest. On this, the Empress Frederick of Germany, who in 1887 as Crown Princess of Prussia had written to her mother, Queen Victoria, of Prince Ferdinand's candidature to the Bulgarian throne, again expressed her opinion about the Prince's ambitions in 1895, saying that: "I am horrified when I read of what Ferdinand is doing in Bulgaria. It seems that he is dying to be recognised by Russia and the other

Powers, and thinks to obtain Russia's favour by all these concessions to the Russophile party, which concessions seem as dangerous to me as they are undignified, and will not buy Russia's good graces one bit, while they do Bulgaria harm." In July 1895, six months after the Empress Frederick had written this letter to her mother, the autocratic Prime Minister of Bulgaria, Stefan Stambulov, who promoted an anti-Russian direction, was assassinated in the Bulgarian capital of Sofia by Macedonians. The Empress Frederick wrote to Queen Victoria of the assassination and its impact on Ferdinand I: "This murder of poor Stambouloff [Stambulov] is a very shocking thing and very bad for Ferdinand. The German papers are down upon him in the severest manner – even too harsh, I should think. Still, if he were wise, he would rush back to Sofia, have a strict inquiry made and the murderers brought to justice (even though they may be in the pay of the Russian Panslavists' Committee). Ferdinand seems bent on coquetting with Russia – in the hopes of being recognised, which he will never be." Ferdinand eventually sought better relations with Russia.

Through the turbulent years of his reign in Bulgaria, Ferdinand acquired a dubious reputation from contemporaries. Sir Frederick Ponsonby, King Edward VII's Assistant Private Secretary, noted of

Ferdinand: "When he recounted his early life, he said that when he had ascended the throne of Bulgaria, he determined that if there were any killing to be done, he would be on the side of the killers and not of the killed." Ponsonby added, that Ferdinand "gave one the impression that he could be capable of any crime…"

Ferdinand of Bulgaria, who possessed a cunning streak, also had the ability to hide his emotions and assume "an impenetrable mask." But when he wished, Ferdinand could also be "frank in the expression of his personal feelings, more genially free-and-easy," a "compound of German steadiness and French *élan*." Ferdinand also loved clothes and precious stones and was inordinately proud of his pale hands. To show off these hands and his precious jewels, Ferdinand wore gem-encrusted rings on his fingers, often flaunting them. Ferdinand throughout his life "carried cut previous stones like loose cash in his pocket. He said they soothed him."

Ferdinand of Bulgaria's flamboyance was in stark contrast with his Greek counterpart, King George I. A contemporary observer remarked that both monarchs liked to be their respective countries' ambassadors. But whereas King George I was modest wherever he went, Ferdinand of Bulgaria, "in his sumptuous saloon-carriage known in diplomatic circles as 'The Bulgarian Foreign Office on Wheels,' presented a veritable apotheosis of ostentatious swagger."

With his large nose, sharp chin, and small eyes, Ferdinand was not considered handsome. Princess Daisy of Pless, who saw Ferdinand frequently, though never actually met him, wrote of his "parchment-like face, long Bourbon nose and keen eyes giving the look of an untamed eagle." According to Queen Marie of Romania, a granddaughter of Queen Victoria and a shrewd judge of character who knew the Prince, Ferdinand was "chameleon-like" and "exceedingly *soigné* as to dress and general elegance, grand seigneur to the point of decadence, sarcastic about himself and others..." Queen Marie admitted that Ferdinand "had a great brain, but not a very nice character." He was a man "who cherishes his enemies more than his friends. He is an actor. He enjoys each role he plays – the benevolent uncle, the sinister old monarch, the scholar." Ferdinand was, in Queen Marie's words, "sharp-witted, all-observing" with a "love of intrigue, which he possessed like a fine art."

Another contemporary royal, Kaiser Wilhelm II, had mocking words about his cousin, whom he referred to derisively as "Petit Ferdinand." But Wilhelm also thought Ferdinand of Bulgaria a dangerous leader who needed to be watched and punished if he fell out of line. In 1898, the German Emperor declaimed that the Russians must "be urged to keep things *quiet* in the Balkans; and above all to hobble that scoundrel [Prince] Ferdinand [of Bulgaria] by his mutton legs. For he *is planning something*, and the House of Coburg reaches far up into the North!" Wilhelm II opined that the Ottoman Sultan "must be encouraged at all costs to keep his European troops ready to fight on the Bulgarian frontier and to strengthen them so as to teach Ferdinand a lesson at once." The Kaiser told Sir Frank Lascelles, the British ambassador to Germany, to watch out for the Bulgarian leader: "I told him that Ferdinand would undoubtedly try to create havoc down there [the Bulgarian frontier]; if he did so and provoked a European conflagration in the process, *I* would *have him murdered without further ado*, for '*fire raisers*' of that kind must be got rid of at once…"

Ferdinand did, indeed, become an active sovereign of his adopted nation and never flagged in his ambitions. In 1906, Sir Frank Lascelles, the British ambassador to Germany, reported back to London to his superior, Sir Edward Grey, of a conversation he had with Kaiser Wilhelm II concerning Ferdinand of Bulgaria:

Prince Ferdinand, whom His Majesty described as the cleverest and most unscrupulous of the Princes who reigned in Europe, had attempted to have a political conversation with His Majesty, who had cut him short by saying that any difficulties he might have with the Sultan [of the Ottoman Empire] were entirely his own fault for not keeping his people in order and preventing them from crossing the frontier into Macedonia, and murdering and pillaging the people there. The Prince was a very ambitious man and hoped to make himself King or Emperor of the Balkans. If he ever succeeded, which however was not probable, the foolish Russians would discover that he had been working all along for himself and not for them. On my asking whether His Majesty thought that the Prince would be tempted to move in the event of the death or serious illness of the Sultan, he replied that it was quite possible. In such a case there might be confusion at Constantinople, which the Prince might think would give him his opportunity.

Ferdinand never flagged in his ambitions for Bulgaria and himself, nor did he shirk from dealing with other European Powers and political figures to gain as much advantage as he could for his adopted country. When Princess Daisy of Pless watched Ferdinand calmly munching away in a restaurant, she wondered "if anyone else present saw in that quiet figure the man who for over thirty years played with Emperors, Kings and statesmen as another man might play chess."

In October 1908, Ferdinand formally declared Bulgaria a kingdom and took for himself the title of 'king' or 'tsar.' Ferdinand harbored grandiose concepts of himself and obsessed over a resurrected Byzantium. In his palace, Ferdinand kept a full-length portrait of himself flamboyantly dressed as a Byzantine emperor. It thus came as no surprise that Tsar Ferdinand I would jump at every opportunity to add territory to Bulgaria at the expense of the Turks, which is exactly what occurred in 1912 with the First Balkan War. In this conflict, Bulgaria, Serbia, Greece, and Montenegro waged war against a weakened Ottoman Empire, which lost the war. Tsar Ferdinand had coveted the city of Salonika and wanted to liberate it from the Ottomans, but the victorious Greeks beat him to it so that by the time Ferdinand arrived there, his contemporary, King George I of the Hellenes, and the Greeks, had already laid claim to the city.

After the Ottoman Empire lost in the First Balkan War, the victors soon quarreled with each other over the spoils. In 1913, Tsar Ferdinand ordered his troops to attack Serbian and Greek forces. Bulgaria, however, lost this Second Balkan War. This led to Bulgaria forfeiting large tracts of land to the victors and destroyed Tsar Ferdinand's hopes of a greater Byzantium under his leadership. Though it was a moment of "black despair," Ferdinand was determined to fight on. "My hour will come," declared the Bulgarian Tsar to King Alfonso XIII of Spain in a moment of grandiose bellicosity: "I shall set fire to the four corners of Europe!"

When World War I broke out in 1914, Bulgaria joined the Central Powers, with Ferdinand convinced that he was on the winning side. With the collapse of the Bulgarian army in 1918, Tsar Ferdinand I abdicated in favor of his son, Boris III, on October 3, 1918. Ferdinand left Bulgaria and lived in exile in Coburg, Germany. The author, Hector Bolitho, in an audience with Ferdinand in 1938, found the former monarch intimidating and embittered about the English, a grievance dating back to when Queen Victoria expressed her disapproval of Ferdinand as being unfit for the Bulgarian throne. As for the Queen's grandson, King George V, Ferdinand's "voice growled with anger" when he complained that the British King had been "very unkind to my person." Bolitho concluded that Ferdinand "who had made such a cult of craftiness and mistrust," also had in him, "kindness and simplicity" but these were qualities "of which he had become afraid." Ferdinand died in Coburg at the age of eighty-seven on September 10, 1948.

Though his reign ended in abdication in 1918, Tsar Ferdinand I of Bulgaria is regarded as having been a successful leader. As one historian has put it, Ferdinand, "made a brilliant success of his reign. For the truth was behind that decorative façade lay a very shrewd mind. Ferdinand of Bulgaria proved himself to be far more intelligent, astute, unscrupulous and tenacious than had ever been credited for. That languid manner masked an iron resolve. Before many years had passed, he was being hailed as 'the new Machiavelli'. It was description that pleased him inordinately. He would probably not even have minded that other, even less complimentary nickname, 'Foxy Ferdy'." And though Tsar Ferdinand I lost his crown, "he had been able to save the monarchy. It would be left to Hitler and Stalin, between them, to destroy that." Ferdinand lived to see the destruction of all he had assiduously worked for. For Ferdinand's last years were beset by tragedy. In 1943, his son, Tsar Boris III, died under mysterious circumstances after a visit to Hitler. In 1945, Ferdinand's other son, Prince Kiril, was shot to death by the communists.

Upon learning of his son's execution, Ferdinand declared that: "Everything is collapsing around me!" The former monarch of Bulgaria also lived to see his young grandson, Tsar Simeon II, deposed in 1946, marking the end of Ferdinand's dynasty in Bulgaria.

Illustrations

KING EDWARD VII.
Born, November 9th, 1841.   Crowned, August 9th, 1902.   Died, May 6th, 1910.

King Edward VII, whose funeral in May 1910 was witnessed by some 2.5 million people and attended by nine reigning monarchs

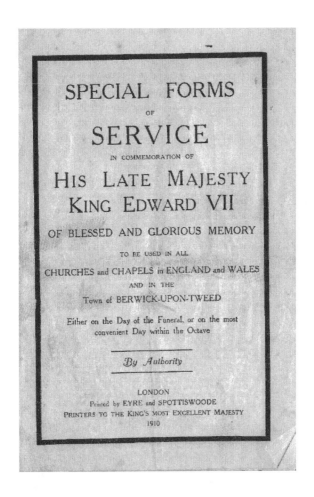

Form of Service used in all churches of England and Wales in commemoration of the late King Edward VII, 1910

The lying in state of the late King Edward VII at Westminster Hall

Caesar, the late King Edward VII's favorite dog

THE FUNERAL PROCESSION OF THE LATE KING EDWARD VII.
THE LATE KING'S CHARGER AND FAVOURITE DOG

Caesar following his master's body at the
funeral procession of the late King Edward VII

THE FUNERAL PROCESSION OF THE LATE KING EDWARD VII
COFFIN ON GUN-CARRIAGE

Funeral procession of the late King Edward VII
– the coffin on the gun-carriage

5 FUNERAL PROCESSION OF HIS LATE MAJESTY KING EDWARD VII.
The Kinh George V., the German Emperor and the Duke of Connaught — LL.

King George V (front center); the late King's brother, the Duke of Connaught (right); and the German Emperor, Wilhelm II (left)

FUNERAL OF KING EDWARD VII
29   H.M. the King of Spain, H.M the King of Norway,
H.M the King of the Hellenes. Friday May 20ᵗʰ 1910. — ND. Phot.

King Alfonso XIII of Spain and to his left, King
George I of the Hellenes

Parade of Kings, London, May 20, 1910

Funeral procession of the late King Edward VII,
London – the Cortege Passing Down Piccadilly

Funeral procession of the late King Edward VII,
Windsor – Royal Mourners at Windsor

Funeral procession of the late King Edward VII,
Windsor – on the Steps of St. George's Chapel

Aerial view of Windsor Castle, on the left is St. George's Chapel

St. George's Chapel on the grounds of Windsor Castle

82.   THE KING AT THE FRONT.
King George and King Albert enjoy an amusing anecdote
Official Photograph—Crown Copyright 101.   "Daily Mail" War Pictures

World War I: Britain's King George V and
King Albert I of the Belgians at the Front

Chapter 7. Kaiser Wilhelm II of Germany (1859-1941)

(reigned 1888-1918)

Wilhelm II of Germany, c. 1902
German Emperor and King of Prussia

The most famous of the nine monarchs on parade at King Edward VII's funeral was undoubtedly the German Emperor and King of Prussia, Wilhelm II, who also happened to have been King Edward VII's nephew. The Kaiser was a regular visitor to England as he was closely related to the British royal family. Throughout his thirty-year reign, Wilhelm II was well-known for his flamboyance and bellicosity. His abdication in 1918 marked the end of the Hohenzollern dynasty's rule over Germany.

****

Kaiser Wilhelm II of Germany was born on January 27, 1859 in Berlin to Prince Frederick Wilhelm of Prussia and his wife, Princess Victoria, the eldest daughter of Britain's Queen Victoria. This meant that Prince Wilhelm had the distinction of being Queen Victoria's eldest grandchild. The Prince's birth had been a difficult and traumatic one and left him with a withered left arm which likely contributed to the future Kaiser's emotional instability. Wilhelm was eventually able to overcome his handicap and could ride a horse with ease and shoot game with skill. Nevertheless, he remained conscious of this smaller, almost useless arm and sought to deflect attention from it. From his birth, Wilhelm was destined to rule Prussia; and during Wilhelm's formative years, Prussia had consolidated power at the expense of other European nations. Thanks to the machinations of Otto von Bismarck, the 'Iron Chancellor,' Prussia emerged after a series of victorious wars to become a power to be reckoned with. In 1871 the German

Empire was proclaimed, with Berlin as the imperial capital. The King of Prussia, Wilhelm I (Prince Wilhelm's paternal grandfather), was proclaimed the new German Emperor (Kaiser) in a ceremony in the Hall of Mirrors at the Palace of Versailles in France.

Within his family, Prince Wilhelm or William, went by the nickname 'Willy.' Willy was a bright child who grew into a complicated adult. Highly-strung and sensitive with a volatile temper, Willy also possessed a strong sense of self-worth, all of which made for a difficult person. Age did not mellow Prince Wilhelm. On the contrary, after he became German Emperor, Wilhelm's outsized personality grew even more overblown. Otto von Bismarck remarked of Wilhelm that: "The Emperor is like a balloon, if one did not hold him fast on a string, he would go no one knows whither."

In 1881, Wilhelm married Princess Augusta Victoria of Schleswig-Holstein-Sonderburg-Augustenburg, who was descended from Queen Victoria's half-sister. Otto von Bismarck had promoted Augusta Victoria as a wife for Wilhelm, ensuring that there would be no foreign influence in the marriage. The pro-English leanings of Wilhelm's mother had injected acrimony in the House of Hohenzollern and Bismarck was keen to see that the future Emperor Wilhelm's consort was

German. In time, Wilhelm and Augusta Victoria became the parents of six sons and a daughter.

As a member of the house of Hohenzollern, Wilhelm was intensely proud of his Prussian lineage and association with the royal house. Being half British, Wilhelm also felt a proud of being partly English. William Boyd Carpenter, the Queen's chaplain and Bishop of Ripon, who knew Wilhelm, noted how: "He found a genuine pleasure in being on English soil, in meeting English friends, and in following English ways. It seemed as though then the spirit of his English ancestry woke and he felt a strong home feeling when he breathed English air."

Wilhelm, however, also felt a distinct antipathy to British liberalism and resented his mother's overtly strong preference for England and all things English. Wilhelm also had an acrimonious relationship with his Uncle Bertie, Queen Victoria's eldest son and heir, the Prince of Wales and future King Edward VII. No such difficulties marred Willy's relationship with his paternal grandfather, Wilhelm I, who lived to a ripe old age and was shy of his ninety-first birthday when he died in in 1888.

Wilhelm I's death meant that the throne passed to his only son who became Emperor Frederick III. Frederick, however, was mortally ill, and died only three months later, making his eldest son and heir, Wilhelm, the new Kaiser in June 1888.

One of Kaiser Wilhelm II's first actions upon acceding to the German throne was to order his soldiers to ransack his parents' palace in Potsdam. The soldiers were told to search for personal papers belonging to his parents which the new Kaiser might use against them – however, anticipating such a move, Willy's parents had left those papers in England, just in case Wilhelm might try and confiscate them. Upon appearing at his mother's home, Wilhelm ignored her and refused to give an explanation for his soldiers' conduct. He had been "very much full of himself, very much the Emperor, playing the bully right and left." Such a callous disregard for his newly widowed mother's feelings was but one glaring example of the Kaiser's cruelty against her. This difficult relationship grew worse through the years, prompting the widowed Empress Frederick to write copious letters of her hurt emotions to her mother, Queen Victoria. In one outburst the daughter lamented to the mother that, "William considers that any public mention of his father's name or mine an offence to him!"

The new German Emperor eagerly embraced his role on the domestic and foreign stage; it could not have been otherwise for Wilhelm II was an impetuous and restless soul. The Kaiser made his presence easily known, laughing with great abandon and mischievously pressing into the hand of those he greeted with his strong right arm. Wilhelm wore rings with the jewels turned inward so that the recipient of his grip would feel the jewels boring into their hand. The Kaiser also had an exaggerated sense of dress. Wilhelm wore military uniforms as a rule and even attended a performance of *The Flying Dutchman* dressed in the uniform of an Admiral of the Fleet. With his quick mind and ability to speak cogently on a variety of topics, Wilhelm had much going for him. Yet as one biographer has noted, this "quickness of apprehension, when combined with his energy and impatience, was more of a liability than an asset."

One of Wilhelm II's closest confidantes, Philip, Prince of Eulenberg, once told Bernhard von Bülow (who served as Wilhelm II's Chancellor from 1900 to 1909) about the Kaiser's difficult personality: "He likes to give advice to others but is unwilling to take it himself … Wilhelm II wants to shine and to do and decide everything himself. What he wants to do himself unfortunately often goes wrong. He loves glory, he is ambitious and jealous. To get him to accept an idea one has to pretend that the idea came from him." Moreover, "if one remains silent when he deserves recognition, he eventually sees malevolence in it." Von Bülow himself discovered Wilhelm II's complicated personality: "I could see that he was endowed with many exceptional gifts, capable in the highest degree of assimilating knowledge of all kinds, full of the best intentions … But as I lived and laboured at his side I saw his faults grow more and more pronounced: an open mind, but one that would never concentrate; a quick, but superficial intelligence, a natural manner, but no tact, with, at times, the lack of all dignity and control. More and more, like quicksands at low tide, the ugly traits began to show themselves – his excessive vanity, näive egotism, lack of discernment, insufficient regard for truth, either with himself or other people."

As his reign unfolded Wilhelm II's autocratic beliefs and tendencies came to the fore. Speeches he gave raised eyebrows such as the one where Wilhelm urged his listeners to follow him on the particular path "which I tread, and which I have marked out for myself, to lead you and all of us towards My goal and towards the salvation of the whole nation…" In another pronouncement, Wilhelm declaimed with pride: "Everything that is finest and best in Germany we owe to the House of Hohenzollern which brought it all about, and so it shall be in my reign too." Such self-aggrandizing and grandstanding, along with his disregard of others' feelings did not sit well with Wilhelm's mother, the Empress Frederick, who wrote to her mother, Queen Victoria: "William has yet to learn that one cannot ride rough-shod over other people's feelings and rights and views, without causing them to rise up and protest and resist such treatment! He is really like a child that pulls off a fly's legs or wings and does not think the fly minds it, or that it matters." Queen Victoria, too, had expressed her indignation at her grandson's overbearing sense of self, writing, "… to pretend that he is to be treated *in private* as in public as 'His Imperial Majesty' is *perfect madness*! … *If* he has *such* notions, he (had) better *never* come *here*."

When Queen Victoria was dying in January 1901, Kaiser Wilhelm rushed to her bedside at Osborne House on the Isle of Wight, uncharacteristically insisting that he was there not as emperor but as a grandson. Wilhelm surprised his British relations with his solicitous attitude toward the aged Queen and when she died, it was in the Kaiser's arms. The death of Queen Victoria meant that Wilhelm's nemesis, his Uncle Bertie, at the age of fifty-nine, had become Britain's King Edward VII.

Both King Edward VII and Kaiser Wilhelm II shared an interest in international affairs. Both men took active roles in promoting their respective countries' interests. But whereas King Edward possessed a charm and sophisticated finesse in dealing with foreign diplomats and leaders, Wilhelm II stood out for his notorious braggadocio. Kaiser Wilhelm envisioned himself a dynamo, all-knowing, a veritable font of wisdom. He liked to insert himself in diplomatic dealings with the European powers. The Kaiser's mother was never impressed with her son's attempts in this arena, for the Empress Frederick knew her son's "idea of diplomacy was to tell one country that the other had secret plans to ruin it, and when they had fallen out to seize what plums he could for Germany." Wilhelm II's meddling in foreign affairs never abated from the time of his accession in 1888. Such behavior was not surprising in a man who liked to see himself as the 'All-Highest.'

With his brash personality, Wilhelm II was not popular with most of Europe's royals. King George I of the Hellenes was one of those who was no fan of the German Emperor. Queen Olga once asked her husband, King George I: "Why on earth do you always go to Corfu [where Wilhelm had a villa] to meet the Kaiser?"

"If I don't, he'll think he's the King of Greece," said King George bluntly.

Tsarina Alexandra of Russia, wife of Tsar Nicholas II, and herself a first cousin of Kaiser Wilhelm, had scathing words to say about the German Emperor. "He thinks himself a superman," the Tsarina declared contemptuously, "and he's really nothing but a clown."

The Kaiser's bombastic personality was fed by the militaristic character of the Prussian court over which he presided. As supreme war lord, the Kaiser not only delighted in holding this title and strutting about in his military uniforms, Wilhelm also encouraged German plans to build up its navy and fulfil its destiny as a great naval power. In so doing, the Kaiser was convinced that Germany could surpass Britain's vaunted Royal Navy. In the waning years of the nineteenth century, tensions between Britain and Germany grew largely because of German desire to expand her fleet. This expansion grew more alarming from 1905 as the German naval build-up proceeded full steam. The German naval arms race sent alarm bells ringing with the British. By the time King Edward VII died in 1910, a strong sense of mutual distrust permeated Anglo-German relations. It did not take a giant leap for this sense of suspicion to poison Wilhelm's views of his Uncle Bertie, views which he had held for years. Edward VII was well aware of this. "I know the German Emperor hates me," the King once admitted candidly to a friend, "and never loses an opportunity of saying so behind my back, while I have always been kind and nice to him."

For the Kaiser, a poseur and actor at heart, tact was never a strong point. Princess Daisy of Pless, who mingled with Wilhelm II, wrote bluntly that, "his tactlessness was appalling." The Kaiser's tactlessness was such that Wilhelm's imprudent behavior had the risk of putting his country's relations with others in peril. He shocked a diplomat with decidedly undiplomatic language when Wilhelm spoke of the diminutive Italian King Vittorio Emanuele III as "the Dwarf" and called his wife, Queen Elena, whose father was King Nikola of Montenegro, "a peasant girl" who was "the daughter of a cattle thief."

Indiscrete and impulsive, the Kaiser was never shy about expressing his enthusiasms and dislikes. This was especially marked when it came to his feelings about his British royal relations, England, and the English. Wilhelm II once told Tsar Alexander III of Russia, that King Edward VII – the Tsar's brother-in-law – had a "false and intriguing nature."

And in another missive, in 1908, the Kaiser declared: "You English are mad, mad as March hares." Wilhelm went on to complain in bitter tones how the English misjudged him. Princess Daisy of

Pless summed up Kaiser Wilhelm's love-hate relationship with England and his English relatives, whom he felt never appreciated him:

> *The Emperor often criticized England; he always did so impatiently or petulantly as one often does when criticizing relations whom one sincerely likes and admires but one feels are at times lacking in understanding or appreciation. That was the real grievance. The Emperor felt that he was never properly understood or appreciated by Queen Victoria, King Edward, King George or the British people.*

The Kaiser was not averse to sharing his negative views of the English with his fellow sovereigns. To Tsar Nicholas II of Russia, Wilhelm II once wrote, "...they are trying hard, as far as I can make out, to find a continental army to fight for their interests! But I fancy they won't easily find one, at least not *mine*!" The Kaiser added in a mischievous and provocative tone, implying that the British were trying to pry Russia away from their ally, France: "Their [the British] newest move is the wish to gain France over from you..." Wilhelm II may have tried to influence the mild-mannered Nicholas II, but he could never succeed in swaying his uncle, King Edward VII, to throw in England's lot with Germany.

The death of his bitter foe and uncle, King Edward VII, was greeted by Wilhelm with some relief and sense of hope. No longer did he have to contend with a respected nemesis on the world stage who stood up to Wilhelm's bellicosity. As one chronicler has put it, "to the Kaiser," Edward VII's death "meant the dawn of universal peace. The odious encirclement of Germany would now cease, and gentle cousin [King] George [V, Edward VII's successor] would listen to William's counsel." Yet there were also genuine feelings of regret on Kaiser Wilhelm's part at the passing of King Edward VII. The late King was the last tangible link for the Kaiser with "the figures which had dominated his early years." And as such, Lord Esher, who was a close associate of King Edward VII, firmly held to the belief that "of all the royal visitors [to King Edward VII's funeral] the only *mourner* was this extraordinary Kaiser." Wilhelm wrote to Theobald von Bethman-Hollweg, his Chancellor, that "at such a moment [as the funeral] one forgets a great deal" and that:

> *I have been allotted as my quarters the very suite of my parents which I often used to play as a little boy and which are famous for their wonderful view over the whole of Windsor Park. All sorts of memories flooded through me as I paced*

about the rooms where I played as a child, lived as a youth and first as grown-up man, then as ruler enjoyed the noble hospitality of the great Queen [Victoria, the Kaiser's grandmother] and all those distinguished men and women who have passed away. They kindle once again my old sense of belonging which binds me so firmly to this spot and which has made the political developments of the last few years so unbearable for me personally. I am proud to be able to call this place my second home, and to be a member of this royal house, for so everybody has treated me in the kindest way. It was very remarkable that when I left Windsor Castle in an open carriage in front of the very crowd which had stood there in silent grief, a sort of electric shock ran through the people as they recognized me. The words 'the German Emperor' went on getting louder until suddenly someone shouted 'Three cheers for the German Emperor', and thereupon a resounding threefold 'hurrah' broke out from the densely-packed masses in all the streets. My eyes were filled with tears and my neighbor, the King of Denmark, said, 'Why are the people here so fond of you?' It is quite extraordinary the way the people give you such an enthusiastic reception in spite of

*their deep grief for dear Bertie.' I think one
can regard this completely spontaneous
demonstration as a good omen.*

A year later, Kaiser Wilhelm II could still
declare himself in sympathy with his mother's
native land. "I was brought up in England, very
largely," he admitted to Theodore Roosevelt in
1911, "I myself feel partly an Englishman. Next to
Germany I care more for England than for any
other country." Then in a strong outburst, the
Kaiser added: "I ADORE ENGLAND!" But then,
Roosevelt noted that Wilhelm II "continued to
speak of England with a curious mixture of
admiration and resentment."

As for Theodore Roosevelt, his opinion of the
Kaiser varied. In 1910, Roosevelt wrote to his wife,
Edith, about Wilhelm II, saying that the Kaiser was
"too strong to allow himself to appear weak, and
too weak to be strong in a really crucial decision.
I'm tremendously disturbed." A year later,
Roosevelt noted that "the Emperor showed an
astonishing familiarity with all contemporary and
recent history of the political and economic kind."
Roosevelt also added that, "in international affairs
he at times acts as a bully, and moreover as a bully
who bluffs and then backs down; I would not
regard him nor Germany as a pleasant national

neighbor. Yet again and again, and I think sincerely for the moment at least, he dwelt to me on his desire to see England, Germany and the United States act together in all matters of world policy."

The outbreak of World War I in 1914, precipitated by the assassination of Wilhelm II's friend, Austria-Hungary's heir, the Archduke Franz Ferdinand, saw Germany as part of the Central Powers, fight against the Allies. The fact that Great Britain fought against Germany infuriated Kaiser Wilhelm. According to his only daughter, Princess Viktoria Luise, the Kaiser "became very angry with King George, who, he believed, had deceived him."

As the war raged, Wilhelm felt optimistic when the German military did well and pessimistic when it did not. Revolutionary fervor finally contributed to Wilhelm II's abdication in 1918 – on the day that would have been King Edward VII's 77th birthday. Of the historic event of his cousin's abdication, King George V, wrote in his diary: "He has been Emperor for just over 30 years, he did great things for his country but his ambition was so great that he wished to dominate the world & created his military machine for that object. No man can dominate the world, it has been tried before, & now he has utterly ruined his Country and himself."

Of the fateful decision to end his reign, Wilhelm wrote to his wife, telling her that, "God's hand lies heavily upon us! His Will be done! So, on [Chief of the General Staff] Hindenburg's advice, I am leaving the army, after fearful mental struggles." Wilhelm signed the letter, "You deeply mortified husband."

The former Kaiser left Germany for exile and lived in Doorn, the Netherlands. In 1922, the widowed former Kaiser married Princess Hermine Reuss and together they lived in a large manor house in Doorn which Wilhelm had purchased in 1919. Wilhelm was not allowed to travel beyond a fifteen-kilometer radius from his home. The former Kaiser preoccupied his time with chopping wood and writing his memoirs. Wilhelm died at Doorn on June 4, 1941 and is buried there.

Unlike his Belgian counterpart, King Albert I, Germany's Kaiser Wilhelm II did not emerge from the First World War with his reputation intact or enhanced. On the contrary, Wilhelm was one of the unfortunate three monarchs present at King Edward VII's funeral who lost his throne. The Duke of Windsor in his memoirs had summed up the fate of Wilhelm II succinctly: "the principal architect of Europe's tragedy, the German Emperor, had become the lonely woodchopper of Doorn."

Chapter 8. King Alfonso XIII of Spain (1886-1941)
(reigned 1886-1931)

King Alfonso XIII of Spain, c. 1916

A nephew by marriage to King Edward VII, King Alfonso XIII of Spain had the rare distinction among his fellow monarchs present at Edward VII's funeral of being born a king. Like his Iberian counterpart, King Manuel II of Portugal, King Alfonso XIII also lost his throne, fleeing Spain for a life of exile in 1931, having reigned for over four decades.

****

King Alfonso XIII was born in Madrid on May 17, 1886, the posthumous son of King Alfonso XII and his widow, Queen Maria Cristina, who had been born an Archduchess of Austria; and so, in Alfonso XIII's veins coursed the blood of the Bourbons and Habsburgs. Shouts of '*viva el rey!*' – 'long live the king!' echoed when it was learned that Queen Maria Cristina had given birth to a boy. King Alfonso himself commented years later of his status at birth: "I became the King at the very moment of my birth, the youngest king ever known in the history of the civilized world." Pope Leo XIII was a godfather to the baby King, a fitting honor as Alfonso was 'the Catholic King of Spain.'

When Alfonso was a child, he made public appearances in his capacity as King of Spain and was dubbed '*el Rey Niño*' – the Boy King. During one such appearance at the Royal Palace in Madrid, the little boy became bored, left his throne where he had been seated and crawled atop a gilt lion nearby.

"You see," he drily commented to a fellow royal years later, "my childish instinct of self-preservation made me realize the safety a lion as compared to a throne." The throne of Spain was not an easy inheritance for young Alfonso XIII. It was, as one of Alfonso's friends, the Marquess of Londonderry, put it, a "difficult and often perilous position" to be in.

Alfonso's indefatigable mother never stopped teaching and lecturing Alfonso on a myriad of subjects in order to prepare him for his role. Even meals were opportunities for Queen Maria Cristina to lecture Alfonso, so that there was hardly a lost opportunity for the King's mother to teach her only son. During Alfonso's childhood years, his mother acted as regent for her son until he came of age at the age of sixteen in 1902. Queen Maria Cristina, an intelligent, cultured woman of good character, saw to it that her child-King was well-educated, insisting that "she herself regularly examined her son's exercises and, at intervals, he had to pass searching examinations in her presence." Alfonso himself admitted that, "even during our meals Mother never stopped lecturing me on the spirit of government. I do not doubt that had a fire threatened the palace, she would have seized upon it as an opportunity for imparting to me additional knowledge and experience."

The royal youth grew into an energetic and athletic man – "tall, thin, with a long face, an aquiline nose, a steady and penetrating glance, a pleasant countenance with a serious expression." Alfonso had "a rare combination of majesty and sympathy" and was called "The Charming King." Speculation soon grew as to who Alfonso's wife and queen might be. His choice eventually fell on a niece of Britain's King Edward VII, Princess Victoria Eugenie of Battenberg, who was a favored granddaughter of Queen Victoria. The wedding in Madrid in May 1906 proved to be a harrowing event. An anarchist threw a bomb at the bridal couple as they rode in their carriage. Several people were killed, and blood soaked the wedding gown of the new Queen of Spain. The horrific event was one of several assassination attempts that King Alfonso XIII bravely faced.

King Alfonso and Queen Victoria Eugenie became the parents of five sons and two daughters. The marriage also brought misfortune, for the specter of the bleeding disease, hemophilia, shadowed the Spanish court, echoing the tragedy in the Russian court of Tsar Nicholas II. King Alfonso's eldest son and heir, the Infante Alfonso, suffered from hemophilia as did his brother, Infante Gonzalo. Like her cousin, Tsarina Alexandra of Russia, who was also a granddaughter of Queen Victoria, Queen Victoria Eugenie turned out to be a hemophilia carrier and so introduced the dreaded bleeding disease into the royal house of Spain. This placed a strain on the King and Queen's marriage, which through the years, deteriorated.

Though their marriage gradually broke down, King Alfonso and Queen Victoria Eugenie remained actively involved in court life. Much formality dominated the court over which King Alfonso presided. William Miller Collier, the American ambassador to Spain from 1905 to 1909, noted that, "the etiquette of the Spanish court has long been universally regarded rigid and frigid, the most formal and formidable, in Europe." But between 1905 to 1909, King Alfonso sought to temper this rigid formality. This was attributed to Alfonso's "own independence of conviction, his fondness for society, his affability, and his eagerness to learn." Moreover, according to Collier, the King was "much influenced by what he saw in England." King Edward VII, it turned out, "was his [Alfonso XIII's] mentor in many matters, and endeavored to follow his political methods and to adopt his habit of frequent visits to his subjects and of acceptance of invitations to their houses for dinners, balls, and other social functions."

Among the social functions Alfonso XIII was assiduous about attending were the *Te Deums* and requiem Masses. When news reached King Alfonso of the double assassinations in 1908 of King Carlos of Portugal and his heir, Prince Luis,

King Alfonso was present at a requiem Mass for them in Madrid. But fears for King Alfonso's safety dominated the day for according the William Miller Collier, "anarchy was rampant in Spain, and it was thought that a veritable epidemic of lawlessness might break out as a result of the outrage in Lisbon." Just how close King Alfonso was to being assassinated in the church was recounted by Collier:

> ... *during the service detectives had arrested an anarchist at the door of the church. He had endeavored to enter dressed as a priest. On his person was found a loaded revolver. Just such an attempt, in this very disguise, had been thought possible, and the parish clergy had guarded against it by agreeing that a certain word of a certain verse of the Gospel for the day should be required as a pass word of every priest and acolyte and choir-boy entering the church. The anarchist could not give it.*

This 1908 incident was the latest attempt to kill King Alfonso, a result in large part of the political and societal instability and friction that marred numerous years of Alfonso's reign. Radicals fomented social unrest in the country resulting in bloody confrontations such as the one that took place in Barcelona in 1909. Anarchists, socialists, and pro-republicans were virulently anti-clerical and anti-monarchists and so posed a near-constant threat to the King and members of the government. This danger resulted in the assassination of one of King Alfonso's prime ministers in 1912. King Alfonso himself avoided yet another assassination attempt in 1913 when he dodged several bullets as the would-be assassin fired directly at the King. Upon regaining his composure, Alfonso reassured the crowd, giving them a military salute and shouted: "Señores, it is nothing – *Viva España!*" Having had a bomb thrown at him at his wedding and shots fired close-range at him, Alfonso XIII declared, "I prefer revolvers to bombs: they do not scatter; you are hit, or you succeed in dodging the bullets. In either case you do not feel responsible for having caused the death of scores of innocent onlookers."

Despite the numerous assassination attempts made on Alfonso XIII, the King remained brave and continued to be imbued with a *joie de vivre*. "He is young and plucky," wrote Princess Daisy of Pless, a friend of the King's, "in some ways such a child, and yet so clever and determined." Winston Churchill, who knew Alfonso, described him as possessing a "natural gaiety and high spirits" with a "boyish merriment and jollity," characteristics Alfonso shared with King Manuel II of Portugal.

In 1910, when King Manuel II of Portugal was overthrown and the establishment of the Portuguese Republic took place, attention shifted to Spain and that monarchy's fate. A contemporary publication declared that some enthusiasts "have predicted the establishment of an Iberian Republic, embracing both countries." But, concluded the publication, "the downfall of Alfonso's throne is extremely improbable" owing to the fact that "conditions in the two countries" had been "radically different." There had been a united front against the monarchy in Portugal, but in Spain, numerous competing political factions made for a disunited front against King Alfonso's monarchy. Time would tell whether this disunited front against the Spanish monarchy would continue as it was or if it would coalesce, spelling serious trouble for King Alfonso XIII.

During World War I, Spain remained neutral. The royal family and country, however, were divided about which side to sympathize with. The British-born Queen Victoria Eugenie naturally sympathized with the Allies while her mother-in-law, Queen Maria Cristina, sided with the Central Powers. As for Alfonso XIII, he once said: "Only I and the mob are for the Allies."

During the war, King Alfonso became something of a good Samaritan par excellence. He had established a Bureau in Madrid's Royal Palace through which countless prisoners of war from various nations were helped. Among the numerous tasks taken on by Alfonso and his Bureau were the repatriation of civilians, the mitigation of punishments meted, and acting as a medium between interred individuals and their families. When necessary, King Alfonso took personal action by appealing to other crowned heads and governments to help those in desperate circumstances. The figures King Alfonso XIII and his Bureau helped are impressive:

> *70,000 civilians and 21,000 were assisted to obtain repatriation; intervention was made in favour of 122,000 French and Belgian, over 8,000 British 6,350 Italian and 400 Portuguese prisoners-of-war. Over 4,000 visits of inspection were made to prisoner-of-war camps. By the end of the war Spain had voluntarily assumed the guardianship of the Diplomatic interests of all the belligerents, including the United States.*

After World War I, Spain's domestic problems continued to grow. The 1920s were especially volatile. Violence was endemic in the country. The

Sindicado Unico, a "notorious secret society" dubbed by *The New York Times* in 1921 as "Spain's Assassinators," was responsible for the murder of another Spanish Prime Minister, Eduardo Dato, in 1921. In recalling that violent era, King Alfonso noted that: "For the next two years it looked as though no government at all existed in Spain. As a constitutional king, I had to follow the decisions of Parliament; I regret to say that the persons chosen by Parliament to head the government were lacking both in courage and in ability." To exacerbate matters, Spain embarked in 1921 on a long, disastrous military campaign in Morocco to hold on to its Moroccan colony, a war that polarized Spanish society.

In 1923 a military rebellion resulted in a military dictatorship under General Primo de Rivera that lasted until 1930. In April 1931, municipal elections in Spain which were seen as a referendum on the monarchy, resulted in a strong showing for the republicans. Chants not of '*Viva el Rey!*' but of '*Viva la Republica!*'resounded in the streets. The speed with which events moved was swift, for "the Republic was proclaimed almost before people realized what was happening." It was a blow to Alfonso, for as Winston Churchill wrote, the King, "having laboured continually and faithfully in its [i.e., that nation's] service, he felt he had deserved its affection." Such sentiments prompted Alfonso XIII to admit with sadness: "I feel as if I had gone to call upon an old friend and found that he was dead." Such sentiments were echoed by a biographer of Alfonso XIII, who wrote:

> ... it became extremely difficult to say why the King had become unpopular. He was certainly popular before the dictatorship [of Prime de Rivera]: he was popular in accepting the dictatorship: nor did he go against the people in letting Primo go, for after order was restored, they wanted a freer rein. But the truth is that even at the time of the Revolution, he was still loved by the people as a whole. The surge of feeling against him was capricious and instantaneous on the part of the crowd, and due to impatience on the part of the so-called intellectuals, who revenged on him the resentment they felt against the dead Minister [Primo de Rivera].

With support for the monarchy having collapsed, King Alfonso chose to go into exile without abdicating. In explaining his decision to leave his country, King Alfonso declared: "I might have used various means to maintain the royal prerogative and fight my adversaries effectively, but I resolutely wanted to eschew a thing that might throw my country-men into a civil and fratricidal war…"

As King Manuel II of Portugal had done in 1910, King Alfonso XIII left his native country for a life of exile abroad. Alfonso XIII's last act as King of Spain – that of vacating his throne – may have avoided civil war in the immediate aftermath of the fateful elections of April 1931. But, as one chronicler of the King's life put it, "the bloodshed his generosity had spared was to come later … there was nothing in Don Alfonso that he did not share with Spain, and his fall was her own doom."

From Spain, Alfonso arrived first in Paris and then in London. In both cities "the King received an ovation which showed that his work for the prisoners of war had not been forgotten." A few weeks after leaving Spain for exile, King Alfonso gave an interview with the media in which he explained that, "I declined the offers made me to remain and rule by force … For Spain I made the greatest sacrifice of my life when I found she no longer desired me … I may have made mistakes sometimes, but in these possible mistakes I have only thought of the welfare of Spain…"

Alfonso's departure from Spain did not halt the political troubles for his country. The brutal Spanish Civil War with its heavy casualties, rent

Spain asunder from 1936 to 1939. The painful memories of that war continued to haunt the Spanish nation well into the following decades. Alfonso XIII's friend, Princess Daisy of Pless, concluded of the King, that he:

> ... *must possess quite unusual qualities to a accomplish all he did in the face of such endless difficulties. He successfully ruled turbulent and distracted Spain for almost thirty years, steered her with honour and profit through the Great War, manfully defended her neutrality and, by his fine work for the prisoners, wounded and missing of all the belligerents, won the admiration of all civilized people. The gratitude owed to him by the world for this service is, I fear, largely forgotten.*

In February 1941, as Alfonso lay dying in the Grand Hotel in Rome, he said to his designated successor, his third son, the Infante Juan, to be brave, adding words on the duty of kings to suffer. On February 28th, just before he died, Alfonso kissed a crucifix and murmured his final words, "*España: Dios mío*" – 'Spain, my God.'

Winston Churchill in summing up King Alfonso XIII of Spain's life, wrote:

> *To be born a king; never to have been anything else but a king; to have*

reigned for forty-six years, and then to be dethroned! To begin life again in middle age under novel and contradicted conditions with a status and in a state of mind never before experienced, barred from the one calling to which a lifetime has been devoted! Surely a harsh destiny! To have given his best, to have presided over his country during all the perils of the twentieth century; to have seen grow in prosperity and reputation; and then to be violently rejected by the nation of which he was so proud, of whose tradition and history he was the embodiment; the nation he had sought to represent in all the finest actions of his life – surely this was enough to try the soul of mortal man.

Chapter 9. King Albert I of the Belgians (1875-1934)

(reigned 1909-1934)

King Albert I of the Belgians, c. 1919

Of the nine monarchs who followed the coffin of King Edward VII, King Albert I of the Belgians was the one who emerged from the Great War with the most respect and prestige. Though his small country, Belgium, suffered great devastation during World War I, and was overrun by the invading Germans, the King's brave conduct during the conflict earned him the sobriquet, 'Albert the Brave.'

****

The fifth child and second son of Prince Philippe, Count of Flanders and his wife, Princess Marie of Hohenzollern-Sigmaringen, Prince Albert was born on April 8, 1875 in Brussels. As a second son, little thought was given that young Prince Albert might succeed to the Belgian throne one day. But the death in 1891 of his elder brother, Prince Baudouin, made Albert second-in-line in the succession. Prince Albert was given a military education at the *Ecole Militaire* for which the sheltered young man was little prepared. His time at the military academy, however, did help to shape the young Prince and prepare him for his future. As heir to the throne, Albert traveled to the Belgian Congo and the United States. He was also completely in the shadow of his Uncle, King Leopold II of the Belgians, who was notorious for treating the Belgian Congo as his personal fiefdom.

Belgium's King Leopold II found his shy and bookish nephew to be a "sealed envelope," someone who was difficult to get to know. Albert "stood in the greatest awe of his imperious uncle." This, along with the Prince's shyness meant that it was difficult for Albert to make impressive public appearances. His speeches as heir were "read with bashful hesitancy, akin to mumbling." There was little in the young Prince Albert to assume that he was destined for greatness.

As he grew older, Prince Albert continued to be serious-minded and reflective. He was also keen to improve the conditions of his future subjects and pursued projects to that end. He also studied ways to ameliorate the lot of the less fortunate. Prince Albert was not just studious, he also liked the outdoors and became a keen mountaineer. It was during a mountaineering visit to Bavaria that he met Elisabeth, Duchess in Bavaria. In 1900, the couple married. They became the parents of two sons and a daughter. Their elder son would become King Leopold III of the Belgians and their daughter would become Queen Marie José, consort of King Umberto II of Italy.

In choosing Elisabeth as his wife, Albert had done well. With her extroverted personality, intelligence, and confidence, Elisabeth provided the right foil to the introverted and diffident Albert. It was Elisabeth who brought Albert's "complex personality to full flower."

In December 1909, Albert became King of the Belgians at the age of thirty-four upon the death of his uncle, King Leopold II. It was not an easy mantle to wear, for Belgium, which gained its independence in 1830, was a country since its beginning, riven with divisions between its Flemish and Walloon citizens. In Albert's lifetime, the Flemish, who spoke a language similar to Dutch, tended to be looked down upon by their compatriots, the Walloons, whose native language, French, dominated much of Belgian life. This strong rivalry between the two ethnic groups grew through the years so that by the time King Albert I began his reign, it was said that, "there were no Belgians, only Walloons and Flemings." King Albert was determined to bridge this divide. "I must from the first be the King of all my people," Albert said, "only that way can I help them feel that we are truly one nation." Thus, in 1909, when he swore his oath as King of the Belgians before Parliament, King Albert I addressed them in French and Flemish. And in a speech in 1910, King Albert "pointed out that everything would be done to secure the equal rights for both the Flemish and French languages."

Another domestic issue that threatened the delicate fabric of Belgian society was the increasing friction between conservatives and liberals, with socialism and republicanism growing in strength. This and the entrenched linguistic divide meant that King Albert had to navigate these competing forces in such a way so as to be a symbol of unity for the fractious nation and not the pawn of competing factions. It was undoubtedly a challenge for the unassuming monarch.

King Albert I was unprepossessing and lacked the swagger found in some of his fellow kings. In fact, "among Europe's more grandiose monarchs, King Albert was very much the odd-man-out." Tall – the King stood 6 feet 4 inches – but plagued with bad eyesight, Albert was also uncomfortable wearing military uniforms. Moreover, he could not give rousing speeches, nor did the King have the gift of small talk. With his *pince-nez* perched on his nose, and his measured way of speaking – one contemporary said that Albert gave "the impression of a man who weighs his words carefully" – the King resembled a studious professor more than a heroic soldier or imposing potentate. Nevertheless, this unpretentious monarch also possessed a strong streak of humanity. When a gardener could not stop showing his deference to his King by constantly bowing, Albert insisted good-naturedly: "My friend, I am only a man like yourself." In sum, King Albert "was a dreamer; an athlete who scoured the country on foot or on horseback, who never shot a pheasant, but who studied plant life and the migration of birds." Pensive and sensitive, "often, before giving an order, he would bury himself in thought as if he were praying."

The king's qualities - "his compassion, his intelligence, his devotion to duty, his quiet strength, his capacity for leadership" – were more in evidence behind the scenes, such as in the council chamber. Because King Albert's good qualities were largely hidden from public view, it made for a marked contrast to see him and Germany's bombastic Wilhelm II together when the Kaiser made an official visit to Brussels in 1910. Wilhelm did not hesitate to tell Albert of his grandiose concepts of himself, his country, and his dynasty. In one exchange, the Kaiser asked the King why he granted so many audiences to his subjects. To which Albert I replied: "My country and I, we make our policy together."

"But we Hohenzollerns," Wilhelm declaimed pompously, "are the bailiffs of God."

Unlike the vainglorious Kaiser, King Albert, his polar opposite, continued to maintain a quiet, dignified demeanor throughout his reign. When the former President of the United States, Theodore Roosevelt, visited Belgium not long after King Albert ascended the throne, he found the King to have been "a thoroughly good fellow, with excellent manners and not a touch of pretension." Roosevelt was also impressed by Queen Elisabeth. The royal couple, in fact, struck Roosevelt as having "led a thoroughly wholesome life."

Unlike his predecessor, Leopold II, King Albert was a diligent monarch who did not overstep his role as sovereign. King Albert periodically reminded his ministers of his adherence to his constitutional role as monarch, saying that, "*Je sui un Roi con-sti-tu-tion-nel*" ('I am a constitutional [as opposed to absolute] King') in his "slow, emphatic fashion." As King of the Belgians, Albert was devoid of arrogance or pomposity. One contemporary royal described King Albert as "a man of such quiet tact and modesty…"

The mettle of this man 'of quiet tact and modesty' was tested severely in World War I. With the outbreak of war in 1914 imminent, and the fate of neutral Belgium, whose neutrality (guaranteed in 1839 by Europe's Powers), hanging in the balance, King Albert wrote to Kaiser Wilhelm II seeking reassurances that Germany would not violate his country's neutrality. In reply, Wilhelm telegrammed: "As the conditions laid down made clear, the possibility of maintaining our former and present relations still lies in the hands of Your Majesty." Angered by this, King Albert, retorted, "What does he take me for?"

Despite his shyness, Albert, possessed common sense, intelligence, a sense of duty, and a resolute streak – qualities which were soon tested to the fore. In August 1914, Germany threw Belgium an ultimatum: surrender or risk invasion. In response, King Albert declared before the Belgian parliament:

> *If a stranger should violate our territory he will find all the Belgians gathered around their Sovereign, who will never betray his constitutional oath. I have faith in our destinies. A country which defends itself wins the respect of all, and cannot perish. God will be with us.*

The Germans invaded Belgium, ushering in years of suffering for the Belgian people as war and deprivation descended upon them. King Albert was no mere figurehead for the Belgian people. As stipulated by the country's constitution, he was commander-in-chief of his military forces. The King accordingly took command of the army, a role Albert took seriously. It was the first time in Belgian history since 1859 that a monarch had gone into battle commanding his troops. Of the nine monarchs present at King Edward VII's funeral, Belgium's King Albert I was the only one who led his troops in combat.

Once Belgium's neutrality had been violated by Germany, King Albert – the soldier king – wasted no time in requesting help from the Allied countries of Britain and France. But for two long weeks, help did not arrive, and King Albert and his troops fought the German forces on their own. Belgium's heroic resistance against the German onslaught earned the country widespread admiration from abroad. France conferred upon the city of Liège, which fell after eleven days of bloody fighting, the prestigious Legion of Honor. The brutal violation of the country's neutrality rallied the Belgian people. In Belgium, recalled Brand Whitlock, the American Minister to King Albert's kingdom, "there was a new spirit of solidarity; the old feeling between the Flemish and Walloons was forgotten. In those fierce fires a nation was being born anew."

From the earliest moments of the war, King Albert exhibited inspiring leadership and level-headedness in thinking out strategies to fight the enemy. A biographer of the King summed up Albert's actions during this difficult time: "He did not waste any energy in denouncing the enemy, still less did he think of revenge. He was like a captain in a tempest whose thoughts are only for his ship and crew. Duty and honour were identical."

To his troops, King Albert exhorted:

Soldiers,

Face the future undaunted, fight on bravely. In the position in which I have placed you, may you look straight ahead, and call him a traitor who speaks of yielding unless a formal order shall have been given.

The time has come, with the help of our powerful allies, to drive from the soil of our beloved country the enemy who has invaded it, regardless of his pledged word and the sacred rights of a free people.

Albert

The heroic stand of 'brave little Belgium' and the country's King were so admired that *King Albert's Book*: *A Tribute to the Belgian King and People From Representative Men and Women Throughout the World* was published in 1914 with contributions from illustrious individuals: statesmen such as the Herbert Asquith, Winston Churchill, and other notables such as Rudyard Kipling, Claude Debussy, Edward Elgar, John Galsworthy, the Aga Khan, Earl Kitchener, Fridtjof Nansen, Jan Paderewski, and William Howard Taft.

In time, Germany occupied most of Belgium, forcing King Albert to fight on in what little was left of unoccupied Belgian territory. It was at La Panne, a corner of Belgium in the north next to France, that King Albert and Queen Elisabeth resided, sharing with the town's residents, their anxieties, fears, and deprivations, and attending Mass on Sundays with them in the little brick church, just like any parishioner. The feeling of being cornered was reinforced not only by La Panne's geographic location, but also by the fact that the King's residence "stood in the midst of a sandy waste where the salt wind never ceased to blow. Before it lay the [North] sea, behind it a battlefield."

Hugh Gibson, the Secretary of the American Legation in Brussels visited King Albert and Queen Elisabeth at La Panne during the war. Gibson recalled the siege atmosphere that pervaded this small corner of Belgium, a view that had been reinforced when Gibson had an audience with the King in his modest home. "Where we sat," wrote Gibson, "we could see the British ships shelling the Germans, and the windows of the dining-room were rattling steadily." As they talked, Gibson was struck by King Albert's sorrowful countenance. "I looked up at him once," recalled Gibson, "but could not bear to do it again – it was the saddest face one can imagine, but not a word of complaint was breathed."

At La Panne, King Albert received a visit as well, in August 1916, from his British counterpart, King George V, who gave his support to the beleaguered King. No such encouragement came from Kaiser Wilhelm I of Germany, who in early 1917, bellowed his opposition to France and to the Belgian King: "No concessions to France, King Albert not to be allowed to stay in Belgium, the Flemish coast must be ours."

Throughout the war years, King Albert along with Queen Elisabeth, who served as a nurse, became potent symbols of resistance and bravery for their subjects. King Albert became in the Great War, "the symbol of a nation's unsullied honor and of his people's force and resistance." True to form, modest as ever, years after the end of the war, King Albert never inflated his role in the conflict, stating simply: "We were cornered into heroism." Years later, Queen Elisabeth told a British visitor that her husband had been during the war, "quite unconscious of shell fire." Of the King's heroism and his modesty, Queen Marie-José of Italy, the daughter of King Albert and Queen Elisabeth, wrote that: "History gratified my father with the title 'King-Knight.' Nothing surprised him more."

At the end of the war, King Albert rode in triumph in Brussels, his capital, a city that "went mad with patriotic enthusiasm." The King had visited Bruges and Ghent, then Brussels to celebrate with, and thank his people. A biographer of King Albert's summed up these entries succinctly, poetically, but also accurately: "The Entry into Bruges had been joyful. The Entry into Ghent had been triumphal. The Entry into Brussels was, as it should have been, an apotheosis."

King Albert I of the Belgians had become 'Albert the Brave' and served his people well. "Without hesitation," recorded one chronicler of the King, "this young and just man went straight where duty called him." And when the four grueling years of war had ended, King Albert had become "the living symbol of heroic Belgium."

Princess Daisy of Pless, a chronicler of royals and contemporary of King Albert, once wrote what constituted greatness in a modern sovereign. The Princess concluded that "in the hour of supreme trial," a monarch should "identify himself completely and unflinchingly with his country's ideal aspirations and its grim determination to win victory through agony and self-sacrifice." In this, King Albert could be said to have truly matched the words with his deeds.

After the war, King Albert again focused his attention to Belgium. He was disappointed to see that the friction between his Flemish and Walloon subjects had again resurfaced. The economic difficulties wrought by the 1929 depression also negatively affected Belgium. King Albert talked of abdicating and retiring with Queen Elisabeth, thus allowing their son, Prince Leopold, and his wife, to shoulder the responsibilities of being Belgium's monarchs. But, as one chronicler of the Belgian monarchy put it, when it came to King Albert and talk of abdication, "he did not mean it; he had become too much a part of Belgium to desert her..."

On February 17, 1934, King Albert set off to Marche-les-Dames in the Belgian province of Namur to do some rock climbing which he so enjoyed. When the King went missing, a search party was sent. The body of King Albert was found hours later. He had fallen and suffered a fatal blow to the head. The dead King's body was returned to his palace. A delicately carved ivory crucifix – a favorite of the King's from workers of the Congo Mission - was placed in his hands. A visitor was moved by the sight and that of "two Little Sisters of the Poor ... kneeling beside him, lost in prayer in the presence of the great King. And on the white sheet there were white lilies, strewed there by the hands of the Queen." The room had been "a soldier's room," one that was "worthy of him."

King Albert was fifty-eight years old when he died and had reigned for twenty-four years, a

King of the Belgians sincerely mourned, loved, and respected by his subjects. He was succeeded by his son, King Leopold III. To the new King of the Belgians, Britain's King George V sent the following message of condolence:

> *It is with the most profound sorrow that I and my people have learnt of the tragic death of your illustrious father, and I hasten to offer our heartfelt sympathy to you and the people of Belgium.*
>
> *The British Empire can never forget the heroic figure whose courage was an inspiration to the Allies throughout the dark years of war, and will join with the Belgian people in mourning the loss of a true friend and ally.*

The famous scientist, Albert Einstein, who was a friend of the Belgian monarchs, wrote to the newly widowed Queen Elisabeth of his sympathy, of "the brutality of the blows inflicted by blind fate." Einstein ended his letter to the Queen, telling her that, "I share your grief with all my heart…"

The news of King Albert I's sudden death shocked the world, but none more so that the Belgian people who were stunned. For a week, all of Belgium nearly stood still. The Belgian nation, as one chronicler recorded, "was paralysed as if the source of her life had dried up."

The late King's body was borne on a gun-carriage through the streets of Brussels on the day of his funeral. It had been a moving spectacle. But it was not the "mournful pageantry" nor the "booming of guns, the tolling of bells" or the "brilliant robes and uniforms" of countless dignitaries, clergymen, and servicemen that stood out. What stood out was "the hush of the crowd, the mark of awe and sorrow even on the faces of children, the women falling on their knees as the gun-carriage approached, bearing the lost leader to his last resting-place, and some stray remarks such as that of the old man who was heard to whisper: *Au revoir, Albert.*"

Chapter 10. King George V of the United Kingdom (1865-1936) (reigned 1910-1936)

King George V of the United Kingdom and the British Dominions, Emperor of India c. 1923

The funeral of King Edward VII was for the new monarch, King George V, a farewell to both his father and sovereign. The funeral also marked the very public debut of a monarch so different in style and character from his predecessor. Quieter, gruffer, and more provincial than Edward VII, George V liked nothing better than shooting game at his beloved Sandringham estate in Norfolk or perusing his outstanding stamp collection, among the best and most valuable in the world. But far from being a country squire, King George V was both king and emperor whose dominions stretched well beyond the small island nation of Britain. Indeed, the sun during George V's reign never set on the British Empire, just as in the time of his grandmother, Queen Victoria. George proved a diligent constitutional British king and by the end of his reign in 1936, King George V had gained the respect of his people.

****

The future King George V was born on June 3, 1865 in London, the second eldest child of the Prince and Princess of Wales (the future King Edward VII and Queen Alexandra). Through his father, Prince George was a grandson of Queen Victoria, and through his mother, George was a grandson of King Christian IX of Denmark. Where Queen Victoria was known as the 'grandmother of Europe,' King Christian IX was also known as the 'grandfather of Europe' thanks to the fact that his descendants, like Queen Victoria's, also reigned over numerous countries. George V was thus related to many of the crowned heads of Europe. Germany's Kaiser Wilhelm II, through George's father, was his first cousin while Russia's Tsar Nicholas II, through George's mother, was also his first cousin.

Prince George and his siblings – an older brother, 'Eddy,' and three sisters (one of whom, Maud, would marry the future King Haakon VII of Norway) – enjoyed a carefree childhood. They were raised largely at Sandringham in Norfolk "under big East Anglian skies, surrounded by nature, lots of servants, and a menagerie of dogs, monkeys, parrots, horses, cattle and sheep, but far away from other children, their father's social set and national events." Prince George's parents did not seek to impose upon their children the kind of intellectually rigorous and rigid childhood which his own father had to endure. Family life for Prince George had been one of "affection, warmth, gaiety, colour." Thanks to this and to George himself, "the son had never given his parents a moment's anxiety except when he was ill."

Prince George emerged from his unintellectual, unremarkable childhood to spend several years in the Royal Navy. Together with his elder brother, George gained valuable lessons while serving in Britain's Royal Navy. Besides allowing him to travel to many foreign ports, Prince George's naval years instilled in him "self-discipline, orderliness and consistency" and "to the end of his life, he was to retain the unswerving sense of duty of a naval officer."

Since he was born and well into his twenties, it was assumed that Prince George, as the Prince of Wales's second son, would likely not become a future king. This changed in January 1892 when Eddy, the Duke of Clarence, died suddenly. Prince George was therefore unexpectedly thrust into Eddy's position as second-in-line to the throne. George's future was sealed. He was destined to be the next reigning sovereign after his father and grandmother, Queen Victoria.

Prince George not only became second-in-line to the throne, he also married his dead brother's fiancée, Princess Mary of Teck, in July 1893. In time, they became the parents of five sons and one daughter. Two sons became kings: Edward VIII (reigned 1936) and George VI (reigned from 1936 to 1952); and a granddaughter became Queen Elizabeth II in 1952.

Created Prince of Wales after his father became King Edward VII in 1901, George with his wife, Mary, paid official visits to Europe, such as the 1906 wedding of King Alfonso XIII of Spain to George's cousin, Princess Ena of Battenberg. The visit had been an eventful one when an assassin nearly killed the bridal couple. "Thank God! Alfonzo and Ena were not touched although covered with glass from the broken windows," wrote Prince George of the frightening incident. "Naturally, on their return [to the Royal Palace], both Alfonzo and Ena broke down ... Eventually we had lunch ... I proposed their healths, not easy after the emotions cause by this terrible affair..." The visit to Madrid was followed by one to Trondheim where George witnessed his sister, Maud, and brother-in-law, Haakon VII, being crowned the King and Queen of a newly independent Norway.

Prince George himself came to the English throne four years later upon the death of King Edward VII in May 1910. In his diary, the new monarch wrote: "May God give me strength & guidance in the heavy task which has fallen upon me." To a good friend, King George V echoed this message in a letter: "I pray to God that He may give me wisdom & strength to try to follow in my father's footsteps & to work for the welfare of our Great Empire."

King George V was fortunate in that once it was learned that he was to be Britain's next monarch after Queen Victoria and her eldest son, George's father prepared his second son for his future role as sovereign. As one contemporary aristocratic chronicler wrote: "The late King [Edward VII], who was in so many ways the most remarkable man of his generation, never felt that jealousy of his heir … He knew very well that … ultimately it would be for the benefit of his kingdom if he showed its future King how he ought to rule."

George V made much more of an effort to identify with his far-flung empire than Edward VII before him who had preferred to focus on Euro-centric issues. In 1911, King George and Queen Mary travelled to India where they participated in the Delhi Durbar, a magnificent occasion where the couple was formally acclaimed Emperor and Empress of India. The magnitude of the meeting can be seen in the fact that at the Durbar Camp was likely the largest camp ever erected, containing tens of thousands of tents that housed 300,000 people. The Delhi Durbar was a magnificent ceremony infused with all the pageant and grandeur of the pre-World War I era. King George V and Queen Mary were resplendent in coronation regalia, the diamonds and precious stones on the Imperial State Crown on the King's head sparkling like fire as the couple received the homage of their Indian subjects. Of the Coronation Durbar, King George wrote that it was "the most beautiful and wonderful sight I ever saw, & one which I shall never forget." The King-Emperor also added that he was "rather tired after wearing the Crown for 3 ½ hours, it hurt my head, as it was pretty heavy…"

But despite this grand occasion that unfolded in India which marked the apogee of empire, King George V was never at home as an imperial monarch. Nor was he anything like his father on the European diplomatic stage. King George did not involve himself in continental politics like his father had. In this, Germany's Kaiser Wilhelm II summed up his cousin, George V, in comparison to King Edward VII. The Kaiser's only daughter recorded that: "My father had manifestly perceived his English cousin did not possess the same political weight as Edward VII. George always considered himself a constitutional Monarch, more a figurehead than a politician, while Edward's influence and power reached considerably far afield."

Unlike Edward VII, George V, who lacked the glamor and charm of his father, did not frequent the fashionable spas of Europe such as Marienbad and mix and discuss politics with monarchs and diplomats, nor did he enjoy holidays in Biarritz, France. George V was simply never at home in the cosmopolitan cities and capitals of Europe. King George, English to the core, preferred above all,

England; especially his country estate of Sandringham. George V was a landed squire at heart and shooting birds on his vast estate was, to him, an ideal way of spending the day. The King was a first-class shot and it was not unusual to find him at Sandringham, or other estates, shooting birds. At a pheasant shoot in 1913 at Lord Burnham's estate in Buckinghamshire, King George V demonstrated his skills with a gun. The King had successfully shot down thirty-nine birds consecutively with thirty-nine cartridges. On that particular pheasant shoot a mere seven guns "accounted for 3,937 birds," and "on another occasion at the same place he [George V] fired 1,760 cartridges from his guns in a single day."

Besides shooting, King George V also enjoyed sailing, as befitting a man of the navy, for "the sea was in his blood." Yet as much as he enjoyed sailing and shooting, it was philately that held a truly special place in George V's heart. Other monarchs may have been great art connoisseurs, but George V was no art lover. Instead, he focused on philately and was responsible for building up the British royal family's impressive philatelic collection, a collection which still continues to be among the world's finest. An example of George's keen interest in philately can be seen when, as Prince of Wales, George ordered his curator of

174

stamps to purchase at auction a very rare stamp. Price was no object. When the gavel fell, the stamp went for an astonishing £1,400. When a courtier told George: "Did you happen to see in the newspapers that some damned fool had given as much as £1,400 for one stamp?"

By way of a reply, George, in a "quiet and restrained voice" said, "I was the damned fool."

This quiet and solitary philatelic pursuit befitted the reserved personality of King George V who had none of the flamboyance or bombast of his contemporaries, Tsar Ferdinand I of Bulgaria and Kaiser Wilhelm II of Germany. Nor was King George an intellectual like King Manuel II of Portugal. A biographer once described King George V as "not a great thinker" but one who "inspires affection in those who work for him" and was without a doubt, "a shrewd judge of character." King George V also had a "simple kindliness" to him. He possessed "intense loyalty" as well as "honesty and devotion to duty." Though he was "sometimes explosive, sometimes indiscreet in his utterances," George V was "fundamentally disciplined" and to those who served him, the King was "a man whom they were proud to serve, a man to whose interests they devoted their lives without question." A close friend of Queen Mary may have found the King "ordinarily not an imaginative man" but he was also "far too constitutional to be moved by party politics, and too fair and open-minded to harbor personal prejudices."

King George V, having served in the Royal Navy was a gruff sailor at heart. He was plain-talking and sometimes acerbic and had retained much of his sailor's talk and love for the sea. Upon his accession, George V proclaimed his appreciation of the navy and stated: "For thirty-three years I have had the honour of serving in the Navy, and such intimate participation in its life and work enables me to know how thoroughly I can depend upon that spirit of loyalty and zealous devotion to duty of which the glorious history of our Navy is the outcome." It thus came as no surprise that when it came time to educating his own sons, George V ensured that three of his four sons were exposed to life with the navy. "Throughout our naval training," recalled King George V's eldest son, King Edward VIII ('David') who became the Duke of Windsor, "it was continuously hammered into our young minds that there were only two ways of doing things – the Navy way and other ways – and all the other ways were wrong." King George V agreed with such thinking. He emphatically once stated of his eldest son, "the Navy will teach David all that he needs to know."

When World War I erupted, the family ties that bound Europe's various royal families were severed as sides were taken, pitting nations and dynasties against each other. King George V's Britain became an enemy of Kaiser Wilhelm II's Germany. During the war, George felt keenly for the sufferings of his soldiers and their families, admitting that, "I have felt the strain of it, as have most people." The King never gave up on the war effort. Two years into the conflict the King noted: "The Country is united & determined to win this war whatever the sacrifices are & please God 1916 may bring us victory & peace..." An early biographer noted that the King "loathed war for what it was in all its hateful implications. He had none of his grandmother's robust Victorian outlook on war. He was a man of peace..." In this long and hard-fought conflict King George V, as a biographer of his has pointed out, "was not either [*sic*] pro-French, pro-Russian, or pro-German: he was undeviatingly pro-British."

Despite his un-swavering loyalty to his native land, King George V, who came from a line of Germanic ancestors, could not escape anti-German sentiment during the war. Attuned to this, King George was astute enough to note that he needed to show that he and his family were more English than their Germanic surname indicated.

When H.G. Wells in 1917 infamously called George V's court "alien and uninspiring," the King angrily retorted, "I may be uninspiring, but I'll be damned if I'm an alien!" In July 1917, King George declared that instead of belonging to the House of Saxe-Coburg-Gotha, henceforth the name of his family and dynasty was to be the House of Windsor – a move that prompted Germany's Kaiser Wilhelm II to make the acerbic comment that he would be off to see 'The Merry Wives of Saxe-Coburg-Gotha' - in reference to Shakespeare's comedy, *The Merry Wives of Windsor*.

One of the great tragedies that came out of the war years was the execution of the former Tsar of Russia, Nicholas II, and his family. George's physical resemblance to his first cousin, the Tsar, was remarked upon in their lifetimes. The two met periodically during family gatherings in Denmark, the native land of their mothers, and in various official royal occasions, the wedding of George in London, being one of them. The friendly relationship between the two monarchs was not enough, however, to save Tsar Nicholas II and his family from being murdered at Ekaterinburg, Russia. Though overtures were made to try and save Nicholas, his wife, Alexandra (also a first cousin of King George V), and their five children, in the end, the former imperial family never left

Russia and met their tragic fate in July 1918. Though concerns for the family's safety had been expressed, King George V did not know that the imperial family would meet such a grisly fate. Much as the King would have liked to have helped the Russian royals, he had also been deeply concerned about the political consequences that would arise should Britain give asylum to the Romanovs. Concerns were raised that helping the Romanovs make their home in England would be a deeply unpopular move in Britain and might incite wide-spread strikes and opposition among the British. Controversy continues to dog the incident with some excoriating King George V for his decision while others have taken a less harsh view on the King's role in denying the Romanovs asylum in England.

The 1920s and 1930s brought fast-moving changes to England – political and social – that the traditionally-minded King George disliked. According to his eldest son, David, King George V, engaged in a "private war with the twentieth century" that he could not win.

In May 1930, on the twentieth anniversary of his accession, King George V wrote to his wife, Queen Mary, who had been a source of support and strength to him: "I can hardly realise that it is twenty years today that dear Papa died, how time flies but what years they have been & what troublous & anxious ones. I do feel grateful to God that he has enabled me to pass through them & I can never sufficiently express my deep gratitude to you, darling May, for the way you have helped & stood by me in these difficult times. This is not sentimental rubbish, but is what I really feel."

When it came to his own sons, George V did not enjoy the same easy relationship he had had with his own father. Despite the differences in characters and styles, Edward VII and George V were fortunate in that father and son could relate to each other – a bond that barely existed when it came to George V and his sons. "The King was proud of his sons," wrote a courtier with close connections to George V and Queen Mary, "but he was often harsh with them simply because he could not bridge the gulf between their generation and his." The King had a particularly difficult and diffident relationship with his eldest son and heir, David, the Prince of Wales, whose obsession with married women, night clubs, and an American divorcee, Wallis Simpson, was a bitter disappointment to the King. Referring to David, George V remarked presciently: "After I am dead, the boy will ruin himself in twelve months." The King's disappointment in his eldest son was such that King George V was said to have remarked that he hoped nothing would prevent his favored grandchild, Princess Elizabeth, from becoming Queen of England someday. As King George V had wished, his granddaughter – who called him 'Grandpapa England' - did indeed become Queen of England as Elizabeth II in 1952.

Nine-year-old Princess Elizabeth witnessed King George V's Silver Jubilee in 1935, attending the service of Thanksgiving in St. Paul's Cathedral in London, along with her younger sister, Princess Margaret Rose, and her parents, the Duke and Duchess of York. So many people packed the streets of London to cheer King George and Queen Mary as they rode in an open carriage from St. Paul's Cathedral back to Buckingham Palace, that the dense crowds rivaled in number of those who had watched King Edward VII's funeral procession twenty-five years before. The enthusiastic cheering touched the King, who always approached his duties as monarch with earnest seriousness. George V had once remarked to a royal relative: "It is one of the greatest responsibilities on earth to be the ruler of the British people."

The Silver Jubilee was one of the few joyous occasions during the King's final years. Of his Jubilee, George V wrote: "The greatest number of people in the streets I have ever seen in my life. The enthusiasm was indeed most touching. I'd no idea they felt like that about me." The King by this time, according to a family friend, "seemed tired and discouraged." This friend added that:

> *I sensed that sometimes he felt bewildered in an epoch which was so alien to his whole mentality. Communism to him was still identified with the horrors of the Russian Revolution; he had a profound distrust of Fascism, even in its diluted form in Italy, and considered Hitler's regime – rightly – a menace to the peace of the world. Most of all he was distressed by the industrial gloom in Britain with its resultant atmosphere of discontent. Loving his people as he did, and especially the plain working man, he was surprised and wounded by the attacks levelled against the Monarchy by some of the socialists.*

Ten months after his Silver Jubilee, an event that was a "deserved if unsought apotheosis," King George V lay dying at his beloved Sandringham. Unlike his uncle, King George I of Greece, who was shot by an assassin, and unlike his cousin, King Frederick VIII of Denmark, who died alone unexpectedly in a public street, or King Albert I of the Belgians who died in a tragic mountaineering accident, King George V's final hours were spent quietly with his family in his favorite home.

Moreover, George V's subjects were given news of his imminent death in a bulletin with the famous line: "The King's life is moving peacefully towards its close." King George V died on January 20, 1936 and was succeeded by his eldest son, David, who became King Edward VIII. King George V's prediction that this son would ruin himself proved prescient. Before the year's end, Edward VIII had abdicated the throne so that he could marry Wallis Simpson, paving the way for the accession of George V's second son, Prince Albert, who became on December 20, 1936, King George VI.

George V had been a successful King of England who, throughout his life, was guided by principles and precepts that reflected his stout English faith. A loyal son of the Church of England, of which he became its titular head upon his accession, George's favorite religious hymns included such traditional ones as: *O God Our Help in Ages Past*; *Holy, Holy, Holy, Lord God Almighty*; and *Nearer to God My Thee*. And on his writing table, King George V always kept a note written in his own hand with a message that clearly resonated with him:

> *I shall journey through this world but once. Any good thing, therefore that I can do, or any kindness that I can show any human being, let me do it now; let me not*

neglect nor defer it, for I shall not pass this way again.

Chapter 11. King Haakon VII of Norway (1872-1957)

(reigned 1905-1957)

King Haakon VII of Norway, c. 1942

O f the nine kings who attended King Edward VII's funeral in 1910, the one who lived and reigned through both World War I and World War II was Norway's King Haakon VII. King Haakon also happened to be

King Edward VII's son-in-law, by virtue of Haakon's marriage to the King's daughter, Princess Maud. King Haakon VII shared with Tsar Ferdinand I of Bulgaria and King George I of Greece, the distinction of being chosen to reign over a foreign land. King Haakon was the father of a King of Norway (his successor, Olav V) and was also the son, brother, and uncle of three Kings of Denmark (Frederick VIII, Christian X, and Frederick IX, respectively). Of the nine sovereigns who attended King Edward VII's funeral in 1910, King Haakon reigned the longest at 52 years. He also was the last of the nine to die, having lived to the age of 85 and dying in 1957.

****

King Haakon VII was born on August 3, 1871 near Copenhagen and named Carl. He was the second son of Crown Prince Frederick of Denmark (who became King Frederick VIII of Denmark in 1906) and his wife, Princess Louise of Sweden. As the grandson of King Christian IX of Denmark, Prince Carl would visit his grandfather's home, Fredensborg, during the summer months where Carl would mix with his numerous royal relations. These included his first cousins, Britain's future King George V, and Russia's future Tsar Nicholas

II, and Greece's future King Constantine I. Among the numerous cousins Prince Carl met up with during these summer visits was Princess Maud of Wales, the youngest child of the Prince and Princess of Wales who later became King Edward VII and Queen Alexandra.

In 1895, Prince Carl and Princess Maud became engaged. Queen Victoria approved the match and telegraphed Maud's parents: "Hope shortly to meet the acquaintance of my future grandson." The couple married at Buckingham Palace in July 1896 and was given Appleton House on the grounds of the British royal family's Sandringham estate in Norfolk, as a present. It was here that the couple's only child, Prince Alexander, the future King Olav V of Norway, was born in 1903.

Upon his marriage to Princess Maud, Prince Carl was intent on continuing his career with the Royal Danish Navy. Events in Europe, however, dashed this hope. In 1905, Sweden and Norway dissolved their 91 year union, leading to the creation of an independent Norway. The hunt for a new monarch for the vacant throne of Norway ended when Prince Carl of Denmark was chosen as the country's new monarch. Carl's pedigree helped his candidature, for he was a royal prince of a Scandinavian country. Moreover, Carl was the son-in-law of the next King of England. Prince Carl was also the nephew of the Dowager Empress of Russia as well as the King of Greece; and his father was the Crown Prince of Denmark. Prince Carl was also relatively young and had a two-year-old son who would be his male heir. There were obstacles, however, to be overcome before Carl could become King of Norway. Carl himself was hesitant about taking on the role as he had been content serving in the Royal Danish Navy. Moreover, his wife, Princess Maud, was keen to live as much as possible in England. A move to Norway would make that more difficult. An acquiescence to the dissolution from Sweden's King Oscar II was also needed, an agreement which King Oscar eventually gave.

Throughout all this, Prince Carl "declined to behave like an adventurer, going to claim a disputed crown like some medieval baron." King Edward VII, a seasoned observer of the European international scene, urged his son-in-law to accept the Norwegian throne, telling him that: "Am quite aware of a double game going on to prevent your going to Norway … I strongly urge that you should go to Norway as soon as possible to prevent some one else taking your place."

King Edward VII's strong and urgent message was driven to a degree by the machinations of his nephew, the German Emperor. Wilhelm II, "bursting with jealousy and viperous insinuations, was pushing a candidate of his own, chiefly, apparently, as a counter to the dynastic ambitions of Uncle Bertie and Aunt Alix!" Wilhelm fulminated about how his uncle was using his influence in the saga of who should be Norway's new monarch, declaring Edward VII, to be the "arch-mischief maker of Europe."

Prince Carl listened to his father-in-law's advice, but Carl also desired that the Norwegian's people's will be a deciding factor in whether or not he would accept the crown of Norway. "Before I go to Norway," Prince Carl said to the Norwegian explorer, Fridtjof Nansen, "I want to know that the Norwegian people want me to come." A plebiscite was thus held in November 1905 on this question. After all, since Carl declared that: "My task must above all be to unite, not divide," in his eyes, it was imperative that there be no question among the Norwegians about him becoming their king. The result of the plebiscite favored a clear win for the monarchy. The new Norwegian royal family departed Denmark and arrived in Christiania, Norway's capital, in November 1905. To bind himself closer to his new subjects, Prince Carl took the name of 'Haakon' thus becoming King Haakon VII; his wife kept her name, Maud; and their son

was re-named, Olav. In succeeding to the throne of
Norway, Haakon shared the fate of his uncle, King
George I of the Hellenes, in that both Danish
princes became reigning monarchs of a foreign land
before their respective fathers became Kings of
Denmark – King Frederick VIII in Haakon's case,
and King Christian IX in George I's case.

King Haakon VII and Queen Maud were
crowned in 1906 in Trondheim's Nidaros
Cathedral, an event attended by Maud's brother, the
future King George V and his wife, Mary. Writing
to her niece, the future Queen Mary, the
redoubtable Grand Duchess of Mecklenburg-
Strelitz, declared herself shocked that the
Norwegian crown had been, in effect, a
"Revolutionary Throne!" This remark stemmed
from the seemingly contradictory thought that a
monarch should have been elected. The Grand
Duchess was dismissive of Haakon, "he making
speeches, poor fellow, thanking the revolutionary
Norwegians for having *elected* him! no really, it is
all too odd!" As for George and Mary being at
Trondheim to witness Haakon's coronation, the
indignant Aunt Augusta fulminated: "A
revolutionary Coronation! Such a *farce, I* don't like
you being there for it … How can a future *K. & Q.
of E.* go to witness a Coronation 'par la grace du

Peuple et de la Révolution'!!! makes me sick, and I should say, *you too*."

In reply to her shocked Aunt Augusta, Princess Mary wrote: "The whole thing seems curious, but we live in *very* modern times."

The German Emperor, Wilhelm II, also had a deprecating opinion of the manner in which King Haakon VII ascended the throne, echoing those of the Grand Duchess of Mecklenburg-Strelitz. Haakon VII was "king by the 'peoples' [*sic*] will," fulminated the Kaiser, and "therefore no better than the president of some republic."

Toward the end of 1906 King Haakon and Queen Maud paid their first official visit as monarchs of Norway. The chosen destination was Maud's beloved England. King Haakon decided upon England when he learned that Kaiser Wilhelm II was planning on inviting him and Maud to make Germany the destination for their first official foreign visit. Haakon did not want Wilhelm to "steal a march on the English" and so announced that the first Norwegian state visit "must be" to England.

Though the Norwegian monarch had been vested with powers, King Haakon reigned in a manner where he did not take sides with various political parties and chose instead to pursue a role in which the crown exercised a unifying role for the country. The royal court which King Haakon presided over was also in keeping with Norway's decidedly democratic air. All titles and privileges had been abolished by the Norwegian parliament in 1821 and such an egalitarian society continued well into the twentieth century. One British courtier found this absence of a Norwegian aristocracy jarring. It was all "so socialistic that a King and Queen seemed out of place." On a visit to Norway, the Infanta Eulalia, a cousin of King Alfonso XIII of Spain, found King Haakon and Queen Maud to have been "simply the first among equals." Their unpretentious court where there was little pomp and formality suited the couple. Upon leaving the country, the Spanish Infanta concluded that, "the democratic Norwegian Court is the nicest in Europe."

Theodore Roosevelt especially liked King Haakon VII, Queen Maud, and young Prince Olav. "They were dears," Roosevelt wrote of his visit to them in Christiania, "we were genuinely sorry, when we left them…" Roosevelt also noted how egalitarian Norway was, stating that, "they have the most genuinely democratic society to be found in Europe." Moreover, King Haakon "took a keen and intelligent interest in every question affecting his people, treated them and was treated by them, with a curiously simple democracy of attitude which was free from make-believe on either side…" In sum, concluded Roosevelt, "staying at the palace was like staying any gentleman's house with exceptionally charming and friendly hosts." Prince Christopher of Greece summed it up succinctly when he described the "simple democratic lives" of King Haakon and his fellow Scandinavian monarchs. Their people, wrote Prince Christopher, "consider their king as the head of a clan rather than as a sovereign."

Such an egalitarian court was in keeping with King Haakon's own personality. His lack of pomposity was evident during a visit he paid to Windsor Castle in November 1925 for the funeral of his mother-in-law, Queen Alexandra. After the funeral, numerous individuals had gathered in a drawing-room. Seeing a "lonely young man standing apart" from other illustrious individuals, King Haakon approached the eighteen-year-old student from Eton, Lord Frederick Cambridge, a nephew of Queen Mary. King Haakon went over to the young man and said simply, "You don't know me. Let me introduce myself. I'm old Norway."

This lack of pomposity on King Haakon's part was such that he once asked his father-in-law's Assistant Private Secretary whether it was a good idea for him as King of Norway to mingle with his subjects on the tramways. This, King Haakon, thought would help counter some of the "republic leanings of the opposition." Sir Frederick Ponsonby replied that he thought it "would be a great mistake as familiarity bred contempt." Ponsonby went on to the add the analogy that "the captain of a ship never had his meals with the other officers but remained quite aloof" in order "to stop any familiarity with them." What the people wanted of their kings, Ponsonby pointed out, was a monarch "with every conceivable virtue and talent. They were bound therefore to be disappointed if they saw him going about like an ordinary man in the street." Haakon VII must have listened to the advice, for Ponsonby declared: "Whether he took my advice or not I never knew, but I do not recall that he ever tried a tram!"

During World War I, Norway remained neutral. However, because Norway had substantial trade with Germany, Norway was caught in the middle between the belligerent nations of Britain and Germany. Norway became economically vulnerable and food rationing was imposed in 1918.

The interwar years were relatively peaceful in Norway in comparison to other monarchical countries such as Spain, which saw the collapse of the monarchy in 1931. By this time, King Haakon had succeeded in gaining the respect and affection of his subjects. He and Queen Maud gained the Norwegians' approval when the couple became avid skiers, a sport well-loved by the people. Their only child, Crown Prince Olav, married in 1929, Princess Martha of Sweden.

In 1938, Queen Maud died suddenly after an operation during a visit to England. King Haakon was stunned by the news and issued a statement: "God has taken the Queen from me this night, and it is a heavy loss for me to bear, though I well understand it is His will. He has taken her because her work is finished, and He has, I know, spared her thus much suffering."

Queen Maud's death spared her from the horrors of World War II. Nazi Germany invaded Norway in April 1940 and in consequence, Norway declared war on Germany. "Poor Charles [Haakon] of Norway," wrote Britain's Queen Mary of her brother-in-law when news of the invasion reached her.

The German envoy to Norway demanded that King Haakon appoint a government under Vidkun Quisling, whose name became synonymous with that of 'traitor.' To this demand, Haakon "flatly refused even to consider." The King may have been "a modest man, but [he was] not a weak one." In facing his Council of State, King Haakon made an eloquent speech detailing his feelings on

JULIA P. GELARDI

this grave moment in Norwegian history, heavy in significance, with countless lives of his countrymen at stake:

> ... For my part I cannot accept the German demands. It would conflict with all that I have considered to be my duty as King of Norway since I came to this country ...
>
> I have desired to create a constitutional kingdom in loyalty to the people whose invitation I accepted in 1905. I cannot depart from that course ... I do not want the decision of the government to be influenced by or based upon this statement. But I have carefully examined my mind and my position, and I find that I cannot appoint Quisling as Prime Minster, a man in whom I know that neither our people as a whole nor its representatives – the Storting – have any confidence at all.
>
> If therefore the government should decide to accept the German demands – and I fully understand the reasons in favor of it, considering the impending danger of war in which so many young Norwegians will have to give their lives – if so, abdication will be the only course open to me. I have come to this conclusion after grave struggles and self-examination. I have wanted to impart this to you that you may be clear about my position...

I do not want my view, which I have been unable to withhold from you, to be decisive for the government. It must make up its mind without regard to my personal opinion. But I believe I am right in giving the government a clear statement as to how I look at the matter.

Years later, King Haakon explained to the American journalist, William Shirer, that he had kept a copy of Hitler's *Mein Kampf* on his desk. "I read it, and reread it, and marked many passages." Then, in a serious tone, Haakon added: "There was one passage that struck me in *Mein Kampf*. It is the one in which Hitler said that no nation which would not fight in self-defence was worthy of survival. That piece clung to my mind, especially in the confusing days just after the Germans came. For I was convinced that if we did not resist the Germans, we well might be destroyed as a people and nation."

The Germans tried twice to convince the sixty-eight-year-old King Haakon and his government to surrender. Twice, the King refused. In retaliation, the Germans tried to massacre the King and his ministers who had sought refuge in the small village of Nybergsund by sending the Luftwaffe to drop bombs. In the mid-1950s, inhabitants of Nybergsund who lived through that harrowing night still told stories of "the King sitting with them in the snow trying to console them while they watched the German barbarians reducing their modest cottages and possessions to ashes."

In June 1940, King Haakon and the royal family were evacuated on a British Royal Navy ship and taken to London. From there, King Haakon broadcast speeches to Norway to buoy his subjects and lend support to the Norwegian Resistance. The symbol 'H7' which stood for 'Haakon VII' was scrawled, painted, scratched, and even etched in snow by Norwegians as defiant gestures against the Nazi occupation of their country. Five years after their evacuation from their country, King Haakon and his family returned to Norway.

For his eightieth birthday, the Norwegian people in gratitude for his many years of service, gave King Haakon a three-thousand-ton yacht. In 1953, Haakon received in audience, William Shirer, who found the King to have shown "a profound grasp of world affairs and displayed a keen intelligence and – always – great wit."

King Haakon VII died on September 21, 1957, at the age of eighty-five and was succeeded by his only son, who became King Olav V. The Norwegians had done well in voting to have Haakon as their monarch, for he served them with devotion and distinction during his nearly fifty-two year reign.

Chapter 12. Epilogue

None of the nine monarchs in attendance in London at King Edward VII's funeral on that sunny, warm May day in 1910 had any idea what fate had in store for them. For King Manuel II of Portugal and his Iberian counterpart, King Alfonso XIII of Spain, both of whom had ascended the throne at very young ages – in King Alfonso's case at birth – their fates turned out to be the loss of their thrones and permanent exile. Such, too, was the fate of Tsar Ferdinand I of Bulgaria and Germany's Kaiser Wilhelm II, two controversial figures whose flamboyance and machinations earned them more approbation than approval.

King George I of the Hellenes had ended his reign at the height of good fortune for Greece, for the country had just captured the coveted city of Salonika in a victorious Balkan war. But an assassin's bullet put an end to King George I's life soon after. King George I's brother, King Frederick VIII of Denmark, had ascended the throne late in life at the age of sixty-two and only reigned for an uneventful six years.

Uneventful was a word that was not synonymous with the life and reign of King Albert I of the Belgians. The unassuming man rose to the occasion and led his people through the bitter and painful years of World War I, emerging as a hero not only to Belgium, but to the world. King Albert I's death in a mountaineering accident was a tragic and dramatic end to that rarest of kings: a military hero who was a loving family man, unblemished in reputation and greatly loved by his people.

Norway had done right in welcoming to their country as monarch of their newly independent nation a Danish prince who associated himself completely with his new country. King Haakon VII served Norway ably through two World Wars; and his long fifty-two-year reign had been a noble attempt at serving his country well.

Britain's King George V, the host to his eight fellow sovereigns at Edward VII's funeral, had also ended his twenty-five-year reign a well-respected king whose monarchy was world's most famous, whose empire was the largest in history, and whose throne, too, was arguably the one which shone with the most luster.

Through the twentieth century, the nine monarchies represented at the funeral of King Edward VII have had wildly differing fortunes. The German and Portuguese monarchies never recovered from their fall; and their respective claimants through the generations have never been able to emulate the fate of the Spanish monarchy. For in 1975, after the death of General Francisco Franco, Spain saw its monarchy return when King Alfonso XIII's grandson, Juan Carlos, ascended the throne as King Juan Carlos I.

The Greek monarchy's fortunes have fluctuated since King George I's assassination. After the King's death, Greece remained a monarchy until 1924. Two referenda were held, one in 1935 and one in 1946, both of which went the monarchy's way. Consequently, the Greek monarchy was restored in 1935; and in 1946, the Greek monarchy was maintained. However, in 1974, the Greek monarchy was officially abolished, ending the reign of King George I's great-grandson, King Constantine II (who married the great-granddaughter of Denmark's King Frederick VIII and is also the brother-in-law of Spain's King Juan Carlos I).

In a curious twist of history, the grandson of Tsar Ferdinand I of Bulgaria, Simeon II (son of Tsar Boris III), who reigned as a minor from 1943 to 1946 (Simeon was born in 1937), returned to Bulgarian politics when he became the Prime Minister of Bulgaria from 2001 to 2005. Today, of the nine monarchies represented in May 1910 at King Edward VII's funeral, only the monarchs of

Belgium, Denmark, Norway, and Britain have enjoyed uninterrupted reigns since 1910.

Did you enjoy this book?

I hope you enjoyed reading this book. If you did, I would be most grateful if you could please post a brief review on Amazon.

Please see my other books on the Royal Cavalcade series as well. I hope you will find another book or several books from the series which you may come to enjoy. I welcome hearing from my readers. You may reach me via my website at: www.juliapgelardi.com.

Endnotes

Chapter 1

"The most remarkable …. city of pageants.": *Longford Journal*, May 28, 1910.

"I was simply …. its many responsibilities.": John Gore, *King George V: A Personal Memoir* (London: John Murray, 1941), p. 247.

"invigorated and refreshed …. bewildering suddenness": William Boyd Carpenter, *Further Pages of My Life* (London: Williams and Norgate, 1916), p. 239.

"a national loss: it stirred our emotions.": *Ibid.*, p. 260.

"an unbroken flood …. as a king": *Ibid.*, p. 241.

"Throughout the whole …. Edward the Confessor.": *Nottingham Evening Post*, 9 May 1910, p. 5.

"he had an …. of them all.": Maurice V. Brett, ed., *Journals and Letters of Reginald, Viscount Esher, Volume 2: 1903-1910* (London: Ivor Nicholson & Watson, 1934), May 7th, 1910, pp. 460-461.

"The place of …. Europe – or any-where": Major Desmond Chapman-Huston, ed., *What I Left Unsaid: By Daisy Princess of Pless* (New York: E.P. Dutton Co., Inc., 1936), p. 108.

"He was rightly .... and fair play.": Alys Lowth, ed., *My Memories 1830-1913 by Lord Suffield* (New York: Brentano's, 1913), p. 355.

"with King Edward's passing .... judgment of men.": Sir Frederick Ponsonby, *Recollections of Three Reigns* (New York: E.P. Dutton & Co., Inc., 1952), p. 382.

"He is a .... Satan he is.": Count Robert Zedlitz-Trützschler, *Twelve Years at the Imperial German Court* (London: Nisbet & Co., Ltd., 1924), p. 178.

"possessor of the .... tongue in Europe": Barbara Tuchman, *The Guns of August* (New York: Library Classics of the United States, Inc., 2012 reprint from 1962), p. 12.

"ceremonial majesty came .... the breath of life.": Gore, *King George V*, p. 433.

"throughout his life .... his own funeral.": Sir Sidney Lee, *King Edward VII: A Biography, Volume II: The Reign, 22nd January 1901 to 6th May 1910* (London: Macmillan and Co., Ltd., 1927), p. 720.

"Crowned heads with ... of the Coronation [of Edward VII].": Philippe Jullian, *Edward and the Edwardians.* Translated from the French by Peter Dawnay (New York: The Viking Press, 1967), p. 292.

"marked, or seemed .... Europe's reigning houses.": Theo Aronson, *Crowns in Conflict: The*

Triumph and the Tragedy of European Monarchy 1910-1918 (Manchester, NH: Salem House Publishers, 1986), p. 2.

"the queue was .... nation's mourning newspapers.": Jane Ridley, *The Heir Apparent: A Life of Edward VII, the Playboy Prince* (New York: Random House, 2013), p. 563.

"This is too awful.": *Ibid.*, p. 563.

"King George drove .... marvelous medieval setting.": Wilhelm II, Emperor of Germany, *The Kaiser's Memoirs: Wilhelm II Emperor of Germany 1888-1918*. Translated by Thomas R. Ybarra (New York: Harper & Brothers, 1922), p. 129.

"a veritable wake": Theodore Roosevelt to David Gray, October 5, 1911 in Theodore Roosevelt, *Cowboys and Kings: Three Great Letters by Theodore Roosevelt* (Cambridge, MA: Harvard University Press, 1954), p. 109.

"Your handshake with .... of my heart,": Viktoria Luise, Duchess of Brunswick and Lüneburg, Princess of Prussia, *The Kaiser's Daughter: Memoirs of Viktoria Luise, Duchess of Brunswick and Lüneburg, Princess of Prussia*, transl. by Robert Vacha (Englewood Cliffs, NJ: Prentice-Hall, Inc., 1977), p. 46.

"a very competent .... regarded as bumptious.": Theodore Roosevelt to David Gray, October 5, 1911 in Roosevelt, *Cowboys and Kings*, p. 110.

"the funeral was …. to collect more.": Jullian, *Edward and the Edwardians*, p. 292.

"The noble thoroughfare …. discharge their thousands.": *Hull Daily Mail*, 20 May 1910.

"… the greatest crushes …. saw nothing more.": *Longford Journal*, May 28, 1910.

"It was terribly …. of the procession.": *Ibid.*

"all ears were …. he had loved …": *Ibid.*

"not only packed …. streets were jammed." *Taunton Daily Gazette*, May 20, 1910.

"the crowd was …. have ever seen.": Ponsonby, *Recollections of Three Reigns*, p. 381.

"At some places …. mass of humanity.": *The Daily Telegraph & Courier*, May 21, 1910.

"came out not …. privileged Civil servants.": *Ibid.*

"Every window …. specially erected stands.": *Lancashire Evening Post*, 21 May 1910.

"one officer, bearing …. before his company.": *Western Daily Press*, 21 May 1910.

"of indescribable magnificence and dignity": *Hull Daily Mail*, 20 May 1910.

"ceremony almost unprecedented …. of Royal obsequies": *The West Coast News*, 23 May 1910.

"Nothing in recorded …. conceivably be surpassed.": *Western Daily Press*, 21 May 1910.

"brilliant, glittering assembly …. the departed Peacemaker.": *The Daily Telegraph & Courier*, May 21, 1910.

"extreme magnificence and .... by the dozen." *Lancashire Evening Post*, 21 May 1910.

"magic, prodigious, superhuman .... of the people.": *The Daily Telegraph & Courier*, May 21, 1910.

"all conversation was .... your arms reversed.": *Ibid.*

"nearly every bell .... tones of sorrow.": *Taunton Daily Gazette*, May 20, 1910.

"Gorgeous uniforms and .... ahead of them.": *The Daily Telegraph & Courier*, May 21, 1910.

"all the grandeur of Royal baldachins.": *Ibid.*

"by Whitehall, the .... were admirable.": *The Annual Register: A Review of Public Events at Home and Abroad for the Year 1910* (London: Longmans, Green, and Co., 1911), p. 124.

"threaded its way .... before their gaze.": *Hull Daily Mail*, 20 May 1910.

"the kingly group .... attracted every eye.": *The Daily Telegraph & Courier*, May 21, 1910.

"the magnificent solemnities .... to be described.": *Ibid.*

"So gorgeous was .... be seen again." Tuchman, *Guns of August*, p. 11.

"a hot and .... massed military bands." Duke of Windsor, *A King's Story: The Memoirs of the Duke of Windsor* (New York: G.P. Putnam's Sons, 1947), pp. 73-74.

"As I rode …. mourning already described.": Wilhelm II, *Kaiser's Memoirs*, p. 130.

"as the sun …. a deep impression.": *Western Daily Press*, 21 May 1910.

"the appearance of …. of the body.": *The Illustrated London News*, May 24, 1910.

"erect and almost …. most intense interest.": *Western Daily Press*, 21 May 1910.

"displayed extraordinary interest …. of the people…": *The Daily Telegraph & Courier*, May 21, 1910.

"of the splendour of the Royal pageant.": *Ibid.*

"The Tribute of Great Kings to a Great King.": *The Illustrated London News*, May 24, 1910.

"the most remarkable …. the world's history.": *Western Daily Press*, 21 May 1910.

"It was the …. has ever seen…": *Taunton Daily Gazette*, May 20, 1910.

Chapter 2

"a wave of ….with stern faces…": *Western Daily Press*, 21 May 1910.

"solemn dirge …. hearth-throbbing cadences.": *The Daily Telegraph & Courier*, May 21, 1910.

"London had taken …. of King Edward.": *Western Daily Press*, 21 May 1910.

"Although the public …. to the military…": *Hull Daily Mail*, 20 May 1910.

"The silence became …. a tremendous emotion.": *The Daily Telegraph & Courier*, 21 May 1910.

"… quite suddenly, the …. to St. George's Chapel.": *Longford Journal*, May 28, 1910.

"Never in the ….began to tell": *Hull Daily Mail*, 20 May 1910.

"beheld a magnificent …. of the Castle": *Western Daily Press*, 21 May 1910.

"Bluejackets [enlisted men of the Royal Navy] dragged it …. even a little eerie.": Windsor, *A King's Story*, p. 74.

"Such a spectacle …. towering medieval fortress…": *The Daily Telegraph & Courier*, 21 May 1910.

"The skirl of …. no other instruments.": *The Illustrated London News*, May 24, 1910.

"Parma violets and …. the dead King.": *The Daily Telegraph and Courier*, 21 May 1910.

"the service proceeded …. of unequalled beauty.": *Western Daily Press*, 21 May 1910.

"Thus it hath ….. of the Garter.": *Ibid.*

"The Kings passed …. his great experience.": *The Daily Telegraph and Courier*, 21 May 1910.

"the saddest and …. deeply felt everywhere.": Dowager Empress Marie Feodorovna to Tsar Nicholas II, undated letter in Edward J. Bing, ed., *The Secret Letters of the Last Tsar: Being the Confidential Correspondence Between Nicholas II*

Last of the Tsars to His Mother Dowager Empress Maria Feodorovna (New York: Longmans, Green and Co., 1934), pp. 253-254.

"By following the .... have gone through.": Tsar Nicholas II to Dowager Empress Marie Feodorovna, undated letter in *Ibid.*, p. 254.

"hatred of funerals and memorial services": Hector Bolitho, *My Restless Years* (London: Max Parrish and Co. Ltd., 1962), p. 150.

"the gathering of .... was truly remarkable...": Ponsonby, *Recollections of Three Reigns*, p. 381.

"of these [monarchs] by .... King of Norway.": *Ibid.*, pp. 381-2.

"calm and contentment .... massing for Armageddon." R.C.K. Ensor, *England 1870-1914* (Oxford: Oxford at the Clarendon Press, 1936), p. 421.

Chapter 3

"brought up under .... even severe training.": 'The New King of Portugal,' *Current Literature*, 44 (March 1908), p. 271.

"which he learned .... favorite steed himself.": *Ibid.*, p. 269.

"an assembly of .... the monarchical regime.": Russell Earl Benton, "The Downfall of a King: Dom Manuel II of Portugal" Louisiana State University Graduate Thesis Dissertation, April 1975, p. 27.

"Too horrible .... for some time.": Gore, *King George V*, p. 222.

"apathetic spectators .... the hearses passed.": *The Illustrated London News*, February 15, 1908.

"brilliant ceremony .... the whole assembly": *The Sphere*, May 16, 1908.

"As a good .... was prosperous.": *The Sphere*, 8 February 1908.

"of all classes .... turbulent city.": *The Sphere*, 20 November 1909.

"extraordinary precautions .... a heavy heart.": *St. Andrews Citizen*, 20 November 1909.

"Nobody in this .... I miss them!": Clara Macedo Cabral, *The Last King of Portugal and Maggs: An Anglo-Portuguese Alliance* (Ceredigion, Wales: The Gomer Press, 2015), p. 7.

"The unfortunate young .... late as possible.": Dowager Empress Marie Feodorovna to Tsar Nicholas II, 30 September 1910 (O.S.), Bing, *Secret Letters of the Last Tsar*, pp. 256-259.

"The collapse of .... time and opportunity.": Henry Paradyne, "The Uncrowning of Manuel," *Harper's Weekly*, October 15, 1910, volume LIV, no. 2808, p. 8.

"Revolution swept the .... an ancient kingdom.": Benton, "Downfall of a King," p. 129.

"Manuel will have .... our best love.": King George V to former Queen Amélie, 16 October 1910, Fernando Amaro Monteiro, *D. Manuel II e*

D. Amélia: Cartas Inéditas do Exilio (Lisbon: Editorial Estampa, 2012), p. 184.

"I am King .... life & spirits.": Winston Churchill to Clementine Churchill, 5 June 1911, Randolph Churchill, *Winston S. Churchill, Volume II: Young Statesman 1901-1914* (Hillsdale, MI: Hillsdale College Press, 2007), p. 353.

"having a schoolboy's love of fun": Prince Christopher of Greece, *Memoirs of H.R.H. Prince Christopher of Greece* (London: The Right Book Club, 1938), p. 101.

"best amateur pianists": *Ibid.*, p. 102.

"It has been .... officers and soldiers...": former King Manuel II to former Queen Amélie, 24 November 1915, Monteiro, *D. Manuel II e D. Amélia*, p. 53.

"the international situation .... takes us seriously.": ex-King Manuel II of Portugal to the Marquess do Lavradio, 8 July 1915, Antonio Cabral, *Cartas d'El-Rei D. Manuel II* (Lisbon: Livraria Popular de Francisco Franco, 1933), pp. 200-201.

"these terrible events .... of poor Nicky...": John van der Kiste, *Crowns in a Changing World: The British and European Monarchies 1901-36* (London: Grange Books, 1993), pp. 128-129.

"We just returned .... my adopted country.": *Ibid.*, pp. 137-138.

"was preparing the …. in this way.": ex-King Manuel II of Portugal to the Marquess do Lavradio, 20 November 1926, Cabral, *Cartas d'El-Rei*, p. 223.

"I always try …. mercy on Portugal!": *Ibid.*

"Handicapped by both …. but an orphan.": Benton, "The Downfall of a King," p. 46.

Chapter 4

"I should like …. had cost him.": Prince Christopher, *Memoirs*, p. 30.

"a crown of thorns.": Theo Aronson, *A Family of Kings: The Descendants of Christian IX of Denmark* (London: Thistle Publishing, 2014; first published 1976), p. 19.

"the Athenians, indeed …. truly enthusiastic welcome.": Sir Horace Rumbold, *Recollections of a Diplomatist, Volume II* (London: Edward Arnold, 1902), p. 124.

"although he loved …. always came first.": Prince Nicholas of Greece, *My Fifty Years* (London: Hutchinson & Co., Ltd., 1926) p. 26.

"predilection for plain …. of his character.": Captain Walter Christmas, *King George of Greece* (London: Eveleigh Nash, 1914), p. 153.

"So enduringly youthful …. they had matured.": Aronson, *A Family of Kings*, p. 214.

"*gamle pølse* …. old pickled pork.": Harold Nicolson, *King George the Fifth: His Life and*

Reign (London: Constable & Co., Ltd., 1952), p. 30.

"day was never .... to be faced." Prince Christopher, *Memoirs*, p. 31.

"in public he .... aspirations, were his.": Aronson, *A Family of Kings*, p. 62.

"The state and .... manipulation and fraud.": Richard Clogg, *A History of Modern Greece* (Cambridge: Cambridge University Press, 1979), pp. 84-85.

"Things were in .... treasury was empty.": Christmas, *King George*, p. 68.

"the thrones of Greece .... unenviable of positions.": Crown Princess of Prussia to Queen Victoria, May 2, 1870, Roger Fulford, ed., *Your Dear Letter: Private Correspondence of Queen Victoria and the Crown Princess of Prussia 1865-1871* (New York: Charles Scribner's Sons, 1971), p. 277

"The King is .... me a misfortune.": Empress Frederick to Queen Victoria, July 9, 1898, Agatha Ramm, ed., *Beloved and Darling Child: Last Letters Between Queen Victoria and Her Eldest Daughter 1886-1901* (Stroud, UK: Alan Sutton Publishing, 1990), p. 216.

"did a great .... streets of Athens.": David Duff, *Alexandra: Princess and Queen* (London: Collins, 1980), p. 204.

"His own position .... not go on.": Sir James Rennell Rodd, *Social and Diplomatic Memories 1884-1893* (London: Edward Arnold & Co., 1922), p. 238.

"We never knew .... our trunks packed.": Prince Christopher, *Memoirs*, p. 113.

"I am my own Ambassador.": Christmas, *King George*, p. 154.

"ornamental figurehead.... of the Hellenes.": *Ibid.*, pp. 154-155.

"Remember England put .... keep him there.": Duff, *Alexandra*, p. 259.

"All his reign .... his life's work.": Prince Nicholas, *My Fifty Years*, p. 233.

"I shall have ... in my old age.": Prince Christopher, *Memoirs*, p. 118.

"a deep-seated aversion .... of a chronometer,": Christmas, *King George*, p. 164.

"George, by the .... into Greek politics." Clogg, *A Short History of Modern Greece*, p. 104.

"The Greek people .... his valuable life.": Rennell Rodd, *Social and Diplomatic Memories*, p. 239.

Chapter 5

"tall and distinguished-looking.": W.R.H. Trowbridge, *Queen Alexandra: A Study of Royalty* (New York: D. Appleton and Company, 1921), p. 52.

"a good soul .... is so stiff.": James Pope-Hennessy, *Queen Mary 1867-1953* (London: George Allen and Unwin Limited, 1959), p. 328.

"pray warn your .... to be firm.": Lee, *King Edward VII, Vo. II*, p. 318.

"liberal tendencies caused .... the late King Christian.": *Cornish & Devon Post*, 10 February 1906.

"were devoted with .... of his kingdom.": *The Scotsman*, 16 May 1912.

"the personality of .... the European public.": *Ibid.*

"anxious for popularity .... to his people.": Aronson, *A Family of Kings*, p. 264.

"editor's terror .... diametrically opposite views.": *Sheffield Daily Telegraph*, 16 May 1912.

"He had .... love for notoriety.": *The Scotsman*, 16 May 1912.

"At first, I .... and few brains.": Ponsonby, *Recollections of Three Reigns*, p.273.

"Certainly .... the King's permission.": *Sheffield Daily Telegraph*, 16 May 1912.

"To the superficial .... democracy of death...": *The Scotsman*, 16 May 1912.

"The sad news .... makes it worse...": Pope-Hennessy, *Queen Mary*, p. 466.

Chapter 6

"festooned with decorations like a Christmas tree.": Aronson, *Crowns in Conflict*, p. 4.

"'his mother's son,' .... true Orleanist stamp.": John A. Macdonald, *Czar Ferdinand and His People* (London: T.C. & E.C. Jack, 1971), p. 83.

"all her will, ... of the Coburgs.": Stephen Constant, *Foxy Ferdinand: Tsar of Bulgaria* (New York: Franklin Watts, 1980), p. 43.

"We hear that .... been thought of ....": Crown Princess of Prussia to Queen Victoria, April 22, 1887, Sir Frederick Ponsonby, ed., *Letters of the Empress Frederick* (London: Macmillan and Co. Limited, 1928), p. 212.

"carried cut previous .... they soothed him.": Constant, *Foxy Ferdinand*, p. 44.

"in his sumptuous .... of ostentatious swagger.": Christmas, *King George*, p. 154.

"parchment-like face, ... an untamed eagle.": Desmond Chapman-Huston, *What I Left Unsaid*, p. 110.

"chameleon-like": Marie, Queen of Roumania, *The Story of My Life* (New York: Charles Scriber's Sons, 1934), p. 502.

"exceedingly *soigné* .... himself and others...": *Ibid.*, p. 500.

"had a great .... monarch, the scholar.": Bolitho, *My Restless Years*, p. 212.

"sharp-witted, all-observing .... like a fine art.": Queen Marie, *Story of My Life*, p. 499.

"Petit Ferdinand": Röhl, *Wilhelm II*, p. 121.

"be urged to .... of at once...": *Ibid.*, p. 987.

"Prince Ferdinand, whom .... him his opportunity.": Sir F. Lascelles to Sir Edward Grey, September 21, 1906, No. 440 in G.P. Gooch and Harold Temperley, eds., *British Documents on the Origins of the War, Volume III: The Testing of the Entente* (London: HMSO, 1928), p. 391.

"if anyone else .... might play chess.": Chapman-Huston, *What I Left Unsaid*, p. 111.

"black despair .... corners of Europe!": Aronson, *Crowns in Conflict*, p. 92.

"voice growled with .... to my person.": Bolitho, *My Restless Years*, p. 216.

"who had made .... had become afraid.": *Ibid.*, p. 217.

"made a brilliant .... nickname, 'Foxy Ferdy'.": Aronson, *Crowns in Conflict*, p. 83.

"he had been .... to destroy that.": *Ibid.*, p. 183.

"Everything is collapsing around me!": Constant, *Foxy Ferdinand*, p. 330.

Chapter 7

"The Emperor is .... one knows whither.": Empress Frederick to Queen Victoria, 1888 in Ponsonby, *Letters of the Empress Frederick*, p. 363.

"He found a .... breathed English air.": Boyd Carpenter, *Further Pages*, p. 289.

"very much full .... right and left.": Daphne Bennett, *Vicky: Princess Royal of England and German Empress* (New York: St. Martin's Press, 1971), p. 264.

"William considers that .... offence to him!": Empress Frederick to Queen Victoria, 1888 in Ponsonby, *Letters Empress Frederick*, p. 361.

"quickness of apprehension .... than an asset.": Michael Balfour, *The Kaiser and His Times* (London: The Cresset Press, 1964), p. 143.

"He likes to .... malevolence in it.": John C.G. Röhl, *Kaiser Wilhelm II: A Concise Life* (Cambridge: Cambridge University Press, 2014), p. 67.

"I could see .... or other people.": Prince Bernhard von Bülow, *Memoirs 1909-1919*, translated by Geoffrey Dunlop (London: Putnam, 1932), p. 290.

"which I tread .... the whole nation...": John C.G. Röhl, *Wilhelm II: The Kaiser's Personal Monarchy 1888-1900*. Translated by Sheila de Bellaigue (Cambridge: Cambridge University Press, 2001), p. 384.

"Everything that is .... my reign too.": *Ibid.*, p. 385.

"William has yet .... that it matters.": Empress Frederick to Queen Victoria, 1888 in Ponsonby, *Letters Empress Frederick*, p. 363.

"… to pretend that …. *never* come *here*.": Balfour, *The Kaiser*, p. 123.

"idea of diplomacy …. could for Germany.": Bennett, *Vicky*, p. 322.

"Why on earth …. King of Greece": Prince Christopher, *Memoirs*, p. 47.

"He thinks himself …. but a clown.": *Wilhelm II, vol. II*, p. 13.

"I know the …. nice to him.": Balfour, *The Kaiser*, p. 296.

"his tactlessness was appalling.": Major Desmond Chapman-Huston, ed., *Princess Daisy of Pless by Herself* (New York: E.P. Dutton & Co., Inc., 1928), p. 257.

"the Dwarf …. a cattle thief.": Balfour, *The Kaiser*, p. 146.

"false and intriguing nature.": E.P.P. Tisdall, *Alexandra: Edward VII's Unpredictable Queen* (New York: The John Day Company, 1953), p. 191.

"You English …. as March hares": Lee, *King Edward VII, Vol. II*, p. 620.

"The Emperor often …. the British people.": Chapman-Huston, *Princess Daisy of Pless*, pp. 263-264.

"…they are trying …. over from you…": Röhl, *Wilhelm II*, p. 984.

"To the Kaiser …. to William's counsel.": Jullian, *Edward and the Edwardians*, p. 292.

"the figures which ….. a good omen.": Balfour, *The Kaiser*, pp. 307-308.

"I was brought …. admiration and resentment.": Joseph Bucklin Bishop, *Theodore Roosevelt and His Time Shown in His Own Letters, Volume 2* (New York: Charles Scribner's Son's, 1920), pp. 253-254.

"too strong to …. I'm tremendously disturbed.": David Pietrusza, *TR's Last War: Theodore Roosevelt, the Great War, and a Journey of Triumph and Tragedy* (Guildford, CT: Globe Pequot, 2018), p. 37.

"the Emperor showed …. and economic kind.": Bishop, *Theodore Roosevelt, vol. 2*, p. 257.

"in international affairs …. of world policy.": *Ibid.*, p. 258.

"became very angry…. had deceived him.": Viktoria Luise, *The Kaiser's Daughter*, p. 82.

"He has been …. his Country and himself.": Gore, *King George V*, p. 308.

"God's hand lies …. deeply mortified husband.": Viktoria Luise, *The Kaiser's Daughter*, p. 138.

"the principal architect …. woodchopper of Doorn.": Windsor, *A King's Story*, p. 73.

Chapter 8

"I became the …. the civilized world.": Grand Duke Alexander of Russia, *Twilight of Royalty*

(New York: J.J. Little & Ives Company, 1932), p. 43.

"You see …. to a throne.": *Ibid.*, p. 44.

"difficult and often perilous position": Marquess of Londonderry Foreword in Mrs. Steuart Erskine, *Twenty-Nine Years: The Reign of King Alfonso XIII of Spain: An Intimate and Authorised Life Story* (London: Hutchinson & Co. Publishers, Ltd., 1931), p. ix.

"she herself regularly …. in her presence.": Princess Pilar of Bavaria and Major Desmond Chapman-Huston, *Don Alfonso XIII: A Study of Monarchy* (London: John Murray, 1931), p. 59.

"even during our …. knowledge and experience.": Grand Duke Alexander, *Twilight of Royalty*, p. 47.

"tall, thin, with …. a serious expression.": Erskine, *Twenty-Nine Years*, p. 63.

"a rare combination …. 'The Charming King.'": *Ibid.*, p. 65.

"the etiquette of …. formidable, in Europe.": William Miller Collier, *At the Court of His Catholic Majesty* (Chicago: A.C. McClurg & Co., 1912), p. 314.

"own independence of …. other social functions.": *Ibid.*, pp. 320-321.

"anarchy was rampant …. not give it.": *Ibid.*, p. 313.

"Señores, it is nothing – *Viva España!*": Pilar and Chapman-Huston, *Don Alfonso XIII*, p. 156.

"I prefer revolvers …. of innocent onlookers.": Grand Duke Alexander, *Twilight of Royalty*, p. 59.

"He is young …. clever and determined.": Major Desmond Chapman-Huston, ed., *Better Left Unsaid: By Daisy, Princess of Pless* (New York: E.P. Dutton & Co., Inc, 1931), p. 248.

"natural gaiety and …. merriment and jollity": Winston Churchill, *Great Contemporaries* (London: Odhams Press Limited, 1937), p. 163.

"have predicted the …. radically different." Paradyne, "The Uncrowning of Manuel," *Harper's Weekly*, 1910, p. 8.

"Only I and …. for the Allies.": Churchill, *Great Contemporaries*, p. 162.

"70,000 civilians and …. including the United States.": Pilar and Chapman-Huston, *Don Alfonso XIII*, p. 190.

"notorious secret society …. Spain's Assassinators": *The New York Times*, March 13, 1921.

"For the next …. and in ability.": Grand Duke Alexander, *Twilight of Royalty*, p. 104.

"the Republic was …. what was happening.": Erskine, *Twenty-Nine Years*, p. 222.

"having laboured continually …. he was dead.": Churchill, *Great Contemporaries*, p. 166.

"it became extremely .... the dead Minister [Primo de Rivera].": Robert Sencourt, *King Alfonso: A Biography* (London: Faber and Faber Ltd., 1942), p. 235.

"I might have ....and fratricidal war...": *Ibid.*, p. 230.

"the bloodshed his .... her own doom.": *Ibid.*, p. 232.

"the King received .... not been forgotten.": Sir Charles Petrie, *King Alfonso XIII and His Age* (London: Chapman & Hall Ltd., 1963), p. 229.

"I declined the .... welfare of Spain...": *Ibid.*

"... must possess quite .... fear, largely forgotten.": Chapman-Huston, *What I Left Unsaid*, p. 109.

"*España: Dios mío*" – 'Spain, my God.': Sencourt, *King Alfonso*, p. 283.

"To be born .... of mortal man.": Churchill, *Great Contemporaries*, p. 159.

Chapter 9

"sealed envelope,": Theo Aronson, *Defiant Dynasty: The Coburgs of Belgium* (Indianapolis, IN: The Bobbs-Merrill Company, Inc., 1968), p. 115.

"stood in the .... akin to mumbling.": John de Courcy MacDonnell, *Belgium, Her Kings, Kingdom*

& *People* (Boston: Little, Brown and Company, 1914), p. 122.

"complex personality to full flower.": Aronson, *Defiant Dynasty*, p. 140.

"there were no .... truly one nation.": Mary R. Parkman, *Fighters for Peace* (New York: The Century Company, 1019), pp. 10-11.

"pointed out that .... and French languages.": *The Annual Register for the Year 1910* (London: Longmans. Green and Co., 1911), p. 355.

"among Europe's more .... much the odd-man-out.": Aronson, *Crowns in Conflict*, p. 25.

"the impression of .... his words carefully": W.P. Cresson, "King Albert of Belgium," *The World's Work*, Volume XXXVIII, May 1919 to October 1919, p. 634.

"My friend, I .... man like yourself.": Aronson, *Crowns in Conflict*, p. 25.

"was a dreamer .... he were praying.": Charles D'Ydewalle, *Albert and the Belgians: Portrait of a King* (New York: William Morrow & Company, 1935), pp. 210-211.

"his compassion, his .... capacity for leadership": Aronson, *Defiant Dynasty*, p. 162.

"My country and .... bailiffs of God.": *Ibid.*, p. 166.

"a thoroughly good .... a thoroughly wholesome life.": Theodore Roosevelt to Sir

George Otto Trevelyan, October 1, 1911 in Roosevelt, *Cowboys and Kings*, pp. 71-72.

"*Je sui un* .... slow, emphatic fashion." Aronson, *Crowns in Conflict*, p. 26.

"a man of such quiet tact and modesty...": Infanta Eulalia of Spain, *Court Life from Within* (New York: Dodd, Mead and Company, 1915), p. 183.

"As the conditions .... take me for?": Aronson, *Crowns in Conflict*, p. 106.

"If a stranger .... be with us.": Parkman, *Fighters for Peace*, p. 17.

"there was a .... being born anew.": Brand Whitlock, *Belgium: A Personal Narrative, Volume I* (London: William Heinemann, 1919), p. 62.

"He did not .... honour were identical.": Emile Cammaerts, *Albert of Belgium: Defender of Right* (London: Ivor Nicholson and Watson, 1935), p. 32.

"Soldiers, Face the .... free people. Albert": Cammaerts, *Albert of Belgium*, p. 129.

"stood in the .... it a battlefield.": D'Ydewalle, *Albert and the Belgians*, p. 165.

"Where we sat .... complaint was breathed.": Hugh Gibson, *A Journal from Our Legation in Belgium* (Garden City, NY: Doubleday, Page & Company, 1917), p. 373.

"No concessions to .... must be ours.": Aronson, *Crowns in Conflict*, p. 141.

"the symbol of .... force and resistance.": Whitlock, *Belgium, Vol. I*, p. 275.

"We were cornered into heroism.": Cammaerts, *Albert of Belgium*, p. 32.

"quite unconscious of shell fire.": Ponsonby, *Recollections of Three Reigns*, p. 483.

"History gratified my .... surprised him more.": Queen Marie-José of Italy, Albert et Elisabeth de Belgique: Mes Parents (Paris: Plon, 1972), p. 282.

"went mad with patriotic enthusiasm.": Lucas Netley, *Albert the Brave: Submitted to and Read by the Adjutant to the Chief of the Late King's Cabinet in Belgium to which have been added two chapters giving a description of the King's tragic death* (London: Hutchinson & Co. Ltd., n.d.), p. 198.

"The Entry into .... been, an apotheosis.": D'Ydewalle, *Albert and the Belgians*, p. 213.

"Without hesitation .... duty called him.": Cammaerts, *Albert of Belgium*, p. 39.

"the living symbol of heroic Belgium.": Cresson, "King Albert of Belgium," *The World's Work*, Vol. XXXVIII, p. 639.

"in the hour .... agony and self-sacrifice.": Chapman-Huston, *Better Left Unsaid*, p. 16.

"he did not .... to desert her...": Aronson, *Defiant Dynasty*, p. 223.

"two Little Sisters .... worthy of him.": D'Ydewalle, *Albert and the Belgians*, p. 273.

"It is with …. friend and ally.": Netley, *Albert the Brave*, p. 249.

"the brutality of …. all my heart…": Queen Marie-José, *Albert et Elisabeth*, p. 408.

"was paralysed as …. had dried up.": Cammaerts, *Albert of Belgium*, p. 473.

"mournful pageantry …. *Au revoir, Albert*.": *Ibid.*, pp. 473- 474.

Chapter 10

"under big East …. national events.": Miranda Carter, *George, Nicholas and Wilhelm: Three Royal Cousins and the Road to World War I* (New York: Vintage Books, 2011), p. 38.

"affection, warmth, gaiety …. he was ill.": Gore, *King George V*, p. 245.

"self-discipline, orderliness and …. a naval officer.": Aronson, *Crowns in Conflict*, p. 33.

"Thank God! Alfonzo …. this terrible affair…": Gore, *King George V*, p. 212.

"May God give …. fallen upon me.": *Ibid.*, p. 237.

"I pray to God ….. our Great Empire.": *Ibid.*, p. 247.

"The late King …. ought to rule.": Radziwill, *Sovereigns and Statesmen*, p. 236.

"the most beautiful …. was pretty heavy…": Gore, *King George V*, pp. 264-265.

"My father had .... considerably far afield.":
Viktoria Luise, *The Kaiser's Daughter*, p. 82.

"accounted for 3,937 .... a single day.": Sir
Charles Petrie, *The Edwardians* (New York: W.W.
Norton & Company, Inc., 1965), p. 101.

"the sea was in his blood.": Gore, *King George
V*, p. 327.

"Did you happen .... the damned fool.":
Ponsonby, *Recollections of Three Reigns*, p. 394.

"not a great .... judge of character.": Bolitho,
My Restless Years, p. 166.

"simple kindliness .... lives without question.":
Gore*, King George V*, pp. 144-145.

"ordinarily not an imaginative man": Jennifer
Ellis, ed., *Thatched with Gold: The Memoirs of
Mabell, Countess of Airlie* (London: Hutchinson of
London, 1962), p. 102.

"far too constitutional .... harbor personal
prejudices.": *Ibid*., p. 170.

"For thirty-three years .... is the outcome.":
Robert Hudson, *George V: Our Sailor King*
(London: Collins' Clear Type Press, n.d.), p. 283.

"Throughout our naval .... ways were wrong.":
Windsor, *A King's Story*, p. 64.

"the Navy will teach David all that he needs to
know." *Ibid*., p. 59.

"I have felt .... victory & peace...": Gore, *King
George V*, p. 292.

"loathed war for .... man of peace...": *Ibid.*, p. 292.

"was not either .... undeviatingly pro-British.": Nicolson, *George the Fifth*, p. 249.

"alien and uninspiring .... if I'm alien!": Duff, *Alexandra*, p. 284.

"private war with the twentieth century": Duke of Windsor, *A King's Story*, p. 292.

"I can hardly .... I really feel.": Pope-Hennessy, *Queen Mary*, p. 548.

"The King was .... generation and his.": Ellis, *Thatched with Gold*, p. 146.

"After I am .... in twelve months.": Elizabeth Knowles, ed., *The Oxford Book of Quotations* (Oxford: Oxford University Press, 2001), p. 334.

"It is one .... the British people.": Prince Christopher, *Memoirs*, p. 161.

"The greatest number .... that about me.": Pope-Hennessy, *Queen Mary*, p. 555.

"seemed tired and .... of the socialists.": Ellis, *Thatched with Gold*, p. 194.

"deserved if unsought apotheosis": David Cannadine, "Rose's Rex," London Review of Books, Vol. 5, No. 17, 15 September 1983.

"The King's life is .... towards its close.": Pope-Hennessy, *Queen Mary*, p. 559.

"I shall journey .... this way again.": Gore, *King George V*, p. 240.

Chapter 11

"Hope shortly to …. my future grandson.": Patricia C. Bjaaland, *The Norwegian Royal Family* (Otta, Norway: Engers Boktrykkeri A/S, 1986), p. 14.

"declined to behave …. some medieval baron.": John van der Kiste, *Edward VII's Children* (Gloucester, UK: Alan Sutton Publishing, 1989), p. 104.

"Am quite aware …. taking your place.": *Ibid.*, p. 104.

"bursting with jealousy …. maker of Europe.'": Tisdall, *Alexandra*, p. 277.

"Before I go …. me to come." William Shirer, *The Challenge of Scandinavia: Norway, Sweden, Denmark and Finland in Our Time* (Boston: Little, Brown and Company, 1955), pp. 105-105.

"My task must …. unite, not divide.": Bjaaland, *Norwegian Royal Family*, p. 20.

"Revolutionary Throne!" …. *very* modern times.": Pope-Hennessy, *Queen Mary*, pp. 407-408.

"king by the 'peoples' [*sic*] …. of some republic.": Lamar Cecil, *Wilhelm II: Emperor and Exile, 1900-1941, Volume II* (Chapel Hill, NC: The University of North Carolina Press, 1996), p. 16.

"steal a march visit 'must be'": Tisdall, *Alexandra*, p. 278.

"so socialistic that .... out of place.": Ponsonby, *Recollections of Three Reigns*, p. 276.

"simply the first among equals.": Eulalia, *Court Life*, p. 180.

"the democratic Norwegian .... nicest in Europe.": *Ibid.*, p. 196.

"They were dears .... and friendly hosts.": Theodore Roosevelt to Sir George Otto Trevelyan, October 1, 1911 in Roosevelt, *Cowboys and Kings*, pp. 76-77.

"simple democratic lives .... as a sovereign.": Prince Christopher, *Memoirs*, p. 272.

"lonely young man .... I'm old Norway.": Bolitho, *My Restless Years*, p. 128.

"republic leanings of .... tried a tram!": Ponsonby, *Recollections of Three Reigns*, p. 277.

"God has taken .... thus much suffering.": van der Kiste, *Edward VII's Children*, p. 178.

"Poor Charles [Haakon] of Norway": Pope-Hennessy, *Queen Mary*, p. 604.

"flatly refused even .... a weak one.": Shirer, *The Challenge of Scandinavia*, p. 36.

"For my part .... people and nation.": *Ibid.*, p. 37.

"the King sitting .... possessions to ashes.": *Ibid.*, p. 40.

"a profound grasp .... always – great wit.": *Ibid.*, p. 105.

Bibliography

Alexander, Grand Duke of Russia. *Twilight of Royalty*. New York: J.J. Little & Ives CompaNew York, 1932.

The Annual Register: A Review of Public Events at Home and Abroad for the Year 1910. London: Longmans, Green, and Co., 1911.

Aronson, Theo. *Crowns in Conflict: The Triumph and the Tragedy of European Monarchy 1910-1918*. Manchester, NH: Salem House Publishers, 1986.

------------------. *Defiant Dynasty: The Coburgs of Belgium*. Indianapolis, IN: The Bobbs-Merrill Company, Inc., 1968.

------------------. *A Family of Kings: The Descendants of Christian IX of Denmark*. London: Thistle Publishing, 2014; first published 1976.

Balfour, Michael. *The Kaiser and His Times*. London: The Cresset Press, 1964.

Bennett, Daphne. *Vicky: Princess Royal of England and German Empress*. New York: St. Martin's Press, 1971.

Benton, Russell Earl. "The Downfall of a King: Dom Manuel II of Portugal" Louisiana State University Graduate Thesis Dissertation, April 1975.

Bing, Edward J., ed., *The Secret Letters of the Last Tsar: Being the Confidential*

Correspondence Between Nicholas II Last of the Tsars to His Mother Dowager Empress Maria Feodorovna. New York: Longmans, Green and Co., 1934.

Bjaaland, Patricia C. *The Norwegian Royal Family.* Otta, Norway: Engers Boktrykkeri A/S, 1986.

Bishop, Joseph Bucklin. *Theodore Roosevelt and His Time Shown in His Own Letters, Volume 2.* New York: Charles Scribner's Son's, 1920.

Bolitho, Hector. *My Restless Years.* London: Max Parrish and Co. Ltd., 1962.

Brett, Maurice V., ed., *Journals and Letters of Reginald, Viscount Esher, Volume 2: 1903-1910.* London: Ivor Nicholson & Watson, 1934.

Cabral, Antonio. *Cartas d'El-Rei D. Manuel II.* Lisbon: Livraria Popular de Francisco Franco, 1933.

Cabral, Clara Macedo. *The Last King of Portugal and Maggs: An Anglo-Portuguese Alliance.* Ceredigion, Wales: The Gomer Press, 2015.

Cammaerts, Emile. *Albert of Belgium: Defender of Right.* London: Ivor Nicholson and Watson, 1935.

Cannadine, David. "Rose's Rex," *London Review of Books*, Vol. 5, No. 17, 15 September 1983.

Carpenter, William Boyd. *Further Pages of My Life*. London: Williams and Norgate, 1916.

Carter, Miranda. *George, Nicholas and Wilhelm: Three Royal Cousins and the Road to World War I*. New York: Vintage Books, 2011.

Cecil, Lamar. *Wilhelm II: Emperor and Exile, 1900-1941, Volume II*. Chapel Hill, NC: The University of North Carolina Press, 1996.

Chapman-Huston, Major Desmond, ed., *Better Left Unsaid: By Daisy Princess of Pless*. New York: E.P. Dutton & Co., Inc, 1931.

---. *Princess Daisy of Pless by Herself*. New York: E.P. Dutton & Co., Inc., 1928.

---. *What I Left Unsaid: By Daisy Princess of Pless*. New York: E.P. Dutton Co., Inc., 1936.

Christopher, Prince of Greece. *Memoirs of H.R.H. Prince Christopher of Greece*. London: The Right Book Club, 1938.

Christmas, Captain Walter. *King George of Greece*. London: Eveleigh Nash, 1914.

Churchill, Randolph *Winston S. Churchill, Volume II: Young Statesman 1901-1914*. Hillsdale, MI: Hillsdale College Press, 2007.

Churchill, Winston. *Great Contemporaries*. London: Odhams Press Limited, 1937.

Clogg, Richard. *A Short History of Modern Greece.* Cambridge: Cambridge University Press, 1979.

Collier, William Miller. *At the Court of His Catholic Majesty.* Chicago: A.C. McClurg & Co., 1912.

Constant, Stephen. *Foxy Ferdinand: Tsar of Bulgaria.* New York: Franklin Watts, 1980.

Cornish & Devon Post, 10 February 1906.

Cresson, W.P. "King Albert of Belgium," *The World's Work*, Volume XXXVIII, May 1919 to October 1919.

D'Ydewalle, Charles. *Albert and the Belgians: Portrait of a King.* New York: William Morrow & Company, 1935.

The Daily Telegraph & Courier, 21 May 1910.

Duff, David. *Alexandra: Princess and Queen.* London: Collins, 1980.

Ellis, Jennifer, ed., *Thatched with Gold: The Memoirs of Mabell, Countess of Airlie.* London: Hutchinson of London, 1962.

Ensor, R.C.K. *England 1870-1914.* Oxford: Oxford at the Clarendon Press, 1936.

Erskine, Mrs. Steuart. *Twenty-Nine Years: The Reign of King Alfonso XIII of Spain: An Intimate and Authorised Life Story.* London: Hutchinson & Co. Publishers, Ltd., 1931.

Eulalia, Infanta of Spain. *Court Life from Within.* New York: Dodd, Mead and Company, 1915.

Fulford, Roger, ed., *Your Dear Letter: Private Correspondence of Queen Victoria and the Crown Princess of Prussia 1865-1871*. New York: Charles Scribner's Sons, 1971.

Gibson, Hugh. *A Journal from Our Legation in Belgium*. Garden City, NY: Doubleday, Page & Company, 1917.

Gooch, G.P. and Harold Temperley, eds., *British Documents on the Origins of the War, Volume III: The Testing of the Entente*. London: HMSO, 1928.

Gore, John. *King George V: A Personal Memoir*. London: John Murray, 1941.

Hudson, Robert. *George V: Our Sailor King*. London: Collins' Clear Type Press, n.d.

Hull Daily Mail, 20 May 1910.

The Illustrated London News, February 15, 1908.

----------------------------------, May 24, 1910.

Jullian, Philippe. *Edward and the Edwardians*. Translated by Peter Dawnay. New York: The Viking Press, 1967.

Knowles, Elizabeth, ed., *The Oxford Book of Quotations*. Oxford: Oxford University Press, 2001.

Lancashire Evening Post, 21 May 1910.

Lee, Sir Sidney. *King Edward VII: A Biography, Volume II: The Reign, 22nd January 1901 to 6th May 1910*. London: Macmillan and Co., Ltd., 1927.

Longford Journal, May 28, 1910.

Lowth, Alys, ed., *My Memories 1830-1913 by Lord Suffield*. New York: Brentano's, 1913.

Macdonald, John A. *Czar Ferdinand and His People*. London: T.C. & E.C. Jack, 1971.

MacDonnell, John de Courcy. *Belgium, Her Kings, Kingdom & People*. Boston: Little, Brown and Company 1914.

Marie, Queen of Roumania, *The Story of My Life*. New York: Charles Scriber's Sons, 1934.

Marie-José, Queen of Italy. *Albert et Elisabeth de Belgique: Mes Parents*. Paris: Plon, 1972.

Monteiro, Fernando Amaro. *D. Manuel II e D. Amélia: Cartas Inéditas do Exilio*. Lisbon: Editorial Estampa, 2012.

Netley, Lucas. *Albert the Brave: Submitted to and Read by the Adjutant to the Chief of the Late King's Cabinet in Belgium to which have been added two chapters giving a description of the King's tragic death*. London: Hutchinson & Co. Ltd., n.d.

'The New King of Portugal,' *Current Literature*, 44, March 1908.

The New York Times, March 13, 1921.

Nicolson, Harold. *King George the Fifth: His Life and Reign.* London: Constable & Co., Ltd., 1952.

Nicholas, Prince of Greece, *My Fifty Years*. London: Hutchinson & Co., Ltd., 1926.

Nottingham Evening Post, 9 May 1910.

Paradyne, Henry. "The Uncrowning of Manuel," *Harper's Weekly*, October 15, 1910, volume LIV, no. 2808, p. 8.

Parkman, Mary R. *Fighters for Peace*. New York: The Century Company, 1919.

Petrie, Sir Charles. *The Edwardians*. New York: W.W. Norton & Company, Inc., 1965.

----------------------. *King Alfonso XIII and His Age*. London: Chapman & Hall Ltd., 1963.

Pietrusza, David. *TR's Last War: Theodore Roosevelt, the Great War, and a Journey of Triumph and Tragedy*. Guildford, CT: Globe Pequot, 2018.

Pilar, Princess of Bavaria and Major Desmond Chapman-Huston, *Don Alfonso XIII: A Study of Monarchy*. London: John Murray, 1931.

Ponsonby, Sir Frederick. ed., *Letters of the Empress Frederick*. London: Macmillan and Co. Limited, 1928.

----------------------------------. *Recollections of Three Reigns*. New York: E.P. Dutton & Co., Inc., 1952.

Pope-Hennessy, James. *Queen Mary 1867-1953*. London: George Allen and Unwin Limited, 1959.

Radziwill, Princess Catherine. *Sovereigns and Statesmen of Europe*. London: Cassell and CompaNew York, Ltd., 1915.

Ramm, Agatha, ed., *Beloved and Darling Child: Last Letters Between Queen Victoria and Her Eldest Daughter 1886-1901*. Stroud, UK: Alan Sutton Publishing, 1990.

Rodd, Sir James Rennell. *Social and Diplomatic Memories 1884-1893*. London: Edward Arnold & Co., 1922.

Ridley, Jane. *The Heir Apparent: A Life of Edward VII, the Playboy Prince*. New York: Random House, 2013.

Röhl, John C.G. *Kaiser Wilhelm II: A Concise Life*. Cambridge: Cambridge University Press, 2014.

--------------------. *Wilhelm II: The Kaiser's Personal Monarchy 1888-1900*. Translated by Sheila de Bellaigue. Cambridge: Cambridge University Press, 2001.

Roosevelt, Theodore. *Cowboys and Kings: Three Great Letters by Theodore Roosevelt*. Cambridge, MA: Harvard University Press, 1954.

Rumbold, Sir Horace. *Recollections of a Diplomatist, Volume II*. London: Edward Arnold, 1902.

Sencourt, Robert. *King Alfonso: A Biography*. London: Faber and Faber Ltd., 1942.

St. Andrews Citizen, 20 November 1909.

The Scotsman, 16 May 1912.

Sheffield Daily Telegraph, 16 May 1912.

Sheffield Evening Telegraph, 15 May 1912.

The Sphere, 8 February 1908; May 16, 1908; 20 November 1909.

Shirer, William. *The Challenge of Scandinavia: Norway, Sweden, Denmark and Finland in Our Time*. Boston: Little, Brown and Company, 1955.

Taunton Daily Gazette, May 20, 1910.

Tisdall, E.P.P. *Alexandra: Edward VII's Unpredictable Queen*. New York: The John Day Company, 1953.

Trowbridge, W.R.H. *Queen Alexandra: A Study of Royalty*. New York: D. Appleton and Company, 1921.

Tuchman, Barbara. *The Guns of August*. New York: Library Classics of the United States, Inc., 2012 reprint from 1962.

van der Kiste, John. *Crowns in a Changing World: The British and European Monarchies 1901-36*. London: Grange Books, 1993.

----------------------. *Edward VII's Children*. Gloucester, UK: Alan Sutton Publishing, 1989.

Viktoria Luise, Duchess of Brunswick and Lüneburg, Princess of Prussia, *The Kaiser's Daughter: Memoirs of Viktoria Luise*,

Duchess of Brunswick and Lüneburg, Princess of Prussia. Translated by Robert Vacha. Englewood Cliffs, NJ: Prentice-Hall, Inc., 1977.

von Bülow, Prince Bernhard. *Memoirs 1909-1919.* Translated by Geoffrey Dunlop. London: Putnam, 1932.

The West Coast News, 23 May 1910.

Western Daily Press, 21 May 1910.

Whitlock, Brand. *Belgium: A Personal Narrative, Volume I.* New York: D. Appleton and Company, 1919.

Wilhelm II, Emperor of Germany. *The Kaiser's Memoirs: Wilhelm II Emperor of Germany 1888-1918.* Translated by Thomas R. Ybarra. New York: Harper & Brothers, 1922.

Windsor, Duke of. *A King's Story: The Memoirs of the Duke of Windsor.* New York: G.P. Putnam's Sons, 1947.

Zedlitz-Trützschler, Count Robert. *Twelve Years at the Imperial German Court.* London: Nisbet & Co., Ltd., 1924.

FURTHER READING

Books on the monarchs who are the subjects of this work are numerous. Below are a several which are well worth reading. Some focus on a particular sovereign, other books delve into several monarchs or dynasties.

Aronson, Theo. *Crowns in Conflict: The Triumph and the Tragedy of European Monarchy 1910-1918*. Manchester, NH: Salem House Publishers, 1986.

------------------. *Defiant Dynasty: The Coburgs of Belgium*. Indianapolis, IN: The Bobbs-Merrill Company, Inc., 1968.

------------------. *A Family of Kings: The Descendants of Christian IX of Denmark*. London: Thistle Publishing, 2014; first published 1976.

Balfour, Michael. *The Kaiser and His Times*. London: The Cresset Press, 1964.

Cabral, Clara Macedo. *The Last King of Portugal and Maggs: An Anglo-Portuguese Alliance*. Ceredigion, Wales: The Gomer Press, 2015.

Cammaerts, Emile. *Albert of Belgium: Defender of Right*. London: Ivor Nicholson and Watson, 1935.

Cecil, Lamar. *Wilhelm II: Emperor and Exile, 1900-1941, Volume II.* Chapel Hill, NC: The University of North Carolina Press, 1996.

Christmas, Captain Walter. *King George of Greece.* London: Eveleigh Nash, 1914.

Collier, William Miller. *At the Court of His Catholic Majesty.* Chicago: A.C. McClurg & Co., 1912.

Constant, Stephen. *Foxy Ferdinand: Tsar of Bulgaria.* New York: Franklin Watts, 1980.

D'Ydewalle, Charles. *Albert and the Belgians: Portrait of a King.* New York: William Morrow & Company, 1935.

Gore, John. *King George V: A Personal Memoir.* London: John Murray, 1941.

Nicolson, Harold. *King George the Fifth: His Life and Reign.* London: Constable & Co., Ltd., 1952.

Ridley, Jane. *The Heir Apparent: A Life of Edward VII, the Playboy Prince.* New York: Random House, 2013.

Röhl, John C.G. *Kaiser Wilhelm II: A Concise Life.* Cambridge: Cambridge University Press, 2014.

--------------------. *Wilhelm II: The Kaiser's Personal Monarchy 1888-1900.* Translated by Sheila de Bellaigue. Cambridge: Cambridge University Press, 2001.

van der Kiste, John. *Crowns in a Changing World: The British and European Monarchies 1901-36*. London: Grange Books, 1993.

Wilhelm II, Emperor of Germany. *The Kaiser's Memoirs: Wilhelm II Emperor of Germany 1888-1918*. Translated by Thomas R. Ybarra. New York: Harper & Brothers, 1922.

.

ABOUT THE AUTHOR

J ulia P. Gelardi is an independent historian. After obtaining a Master of Arts degree from Simon Fraser University in Canada, Julia has written books and articles focusing on European royalty that include: *Born to Rule*, *In Triumph's Wake*, and *From Splendor to Revolution*. Having lived in the U.K., Canada, and several states in the U.S., she currently resides in Minnesota with her husband. Here is her webpage: juliapgelardi.com.

OTHER BOOKS BY THE AUTHOR

St. Martin's Press:

Born to Rule: Five Reigning Consorts, Granddaughters of Queen Victoria (2005)

In Triumph's Wake: Royal Mothers, Tragic Daughters, and the Price They Paid for Glory (2009)

From Splendor to Revolution: The Romanov Women, 1847-1928 (2011)

Royal Cavalcade Series:

A Guarded Secret – Tsar Nicholas II, Tsarina Alexandra and Tsarevich Alexei's Hemophilia (2019)

Drina & Lilibet – Queen Victoria and Queen Elizabeth II From Birth to Accession (2019)

<u>Illustration Sources</u>

Cover: The Nine Monarchs at Windsor Castle, May 20, 1910:

Photographed by W. & D. Downey., The Nine Sovereigns at Windsor for the funeral of King Edward VII, marked as public domain, more details on Wikimedia Commons

Introduction, The Nine Monarchs at Windsor Castle, May 20, 1910:

Photographed by W. & D. Downey., The Nine Sovereigns at Windsor for the funeral of King Edward VII, marked as public domain, more details on Wikimedia Commons

Chapter 1, Procession of Nine Kings:

Leonard Bentley, The Funeral of King Edward VII (16566590837), CC BY-SA 2.0

Chapter 2, Funeral procession of the late King Edward VII, London, the Royal Carriages:

Bain News Service, publisher, The funeral procession of the Late King Edward VII. the royal carriages. LCCN2014688207, marked as public domain, more details on Wikimedia Commons

Chapter 3, King Manuel II of Portugal:

Postcard, Edição Costa, R. do Ouro, Lisbon, public domain

Chapter 4, King Frederick VIII of Denmark:

George Grantham Bain Collection (Library of Congress), Frederik VIII of Denmark 1909, marked as public domain, more details on Wikimedia Commons

Chapter 5, King George I of Greece:

J. Beagles & Co. postcard, public domain

Chapter 6, Tsar Ferdinand I of Bulgaria:
Attribution: Unknown, Zar Ferdinand Bulgarien, marked as public domain, more details on Wikimedia Commons

Chapter 7, Kaiser Wilhelm II of Germany:
Voigt   T. H.
(https://commons.wikimedia.org/wiki/File:Kaiser_Wilhelm_II_of_Germany_ -_1902.jpg), „Kaiser Wilhelm II of Germany - 1902", marked as public domain,   more   details   on   Wikimedia   Commons: https://commons.wikimedia.org/wiki/Template:PD-UKGov

Chapter 8, King Alfonso XIII of Spain:
Attribution: Kaulak creator QS:P170,Q5958697, Rey Alfonso XIII de España, by Kaulak, marked as public domain, more details on Wikimedia Commons

Chapter 9, King Albert I of the Belgians:
Attribution: Richard N. Speaight creator QS:P170,Q19999752, Portrait of Albert I of Belgium, marked as public domain, more details on Wikimedia Commons

Chapter 10, King George V of the United Kingdom:
Bain News Service, publisher, Kinggeorgev1923, marked as public domain, more details on Wikimedia Commons

Chapter 11, King Haakon VII of Norway:
unknown, Eneret Mittet & Co. No. 50, Haakon VII FSA, marked as public domain, more details on Wikimedia Commons

Illustrations Section:
London:
King Edward VII, whose funeral in May 1910 was witnessed by some 2.5 million people and attended by nine reigning monarchs:

Photo W.S. Stuart, Valentine's Series, public domain

Form of Service used in all churches of England and Wales in commemoration of the late King Edward VII, 1910:
Public domain

The lying in state of the late King Edward VII at Westminster:
Rotary Photographic Series, public domain

Caesar the late King Edward's favorite dog:
Rotary Photographic Series, public domain

Caesar following his master's body at the funeral procession of the late King Edward VII:
Specific author unknown., Edward VII Funeral Charger and Caesar, marked as public domain, more details on Wikimedia Commons

Funeral procession of the late King Edward VII, London – the coffin on the gun-carriage:
Bain News Service, publisher, The funeral procession of the Late King Edward VII. Coffin on gun-carriage. LCCN2014688204, marked as public domain, more details on Wikimedia Commons

King George V; the late King's brother, the Duke of Connaught; and the German Emperor, Wilhelm II:
Postcard, public domain

Funeral procession of the late King Edward VII, London – the Kings of Spain, Norway, and the Hellenes:
Postcard, public domain

Funeral procession of the late King Edward VII, London – King George V, the German Emperor and the Duke of Connaught:
Postcard, public domain

King Alfonso XIII of Spain and to his left, King George I of the Hellenes:
Postcard, public domain

Parade of Kings, London, May 20, 1910:
Postcard, public domain

Funeral procession of the late King Edward VII, London – the Cortege Passing Down Piccadilly:
Beagles Postcard, public domain

World War I: King George V and King Albert of the Belgians at the Front:
Daily Mail War Pictures Postcard, public domain

Windsor Castle:

Funeral procession of the late King Edward VII, Windsor – Royal Mourners at Windsor:
Rotary Photographic Series, public domain

Funeral procession of the late King Edward VII, Windsor – on the Steps of St. George's Chapel:
Royal Photographic Series, public domain

Aerial View of Windsor Castle:
Mark S Jobling, Windsor Castle from the air, CC BY-SA 3.0

St. George's Chapel:
Aurelien Guichard from London, United Kingdom (changes by Rabanus Flavus), St. Georges Chapel, Windsor Castle (2), CC BY-SA 2.0

Made in the USA
Columbia, SC
24 December 2019

85741833R10141